AF355050

FOWLER'S NET

Vidar Hebek & Rune Larsen

Introduction

Our soul is escaped as a bird out of the
snare of the fowlers; the snare is broken,
and we are escaped.
Our help is in the name of the Lord,
who made heaven and earth.

Psalms 124. 7-8

Preface

It is three issues, and I am familiar with all of them. No excuse. Some never learn. We are like us.

"Ever learning and never able to come to the knowledge of the truth."

My life has been tattooed into my mind and soul - three issues; Manipulating Heros, Depression, and Addiction. A numbered order does not follow it. But each story as it told.

It is is not an essential testimony but mostly revelations. It's to be revealed.

For me, it is a cause of mine. For another is a cause from another.

One thing for sure, is to die from yourself. A learning process to become a new creation.

And become able to stand on the day of judgment.

Never forget the freedom that is given. Free indeed; is from Jesus Christ.

But wrong choices, wrong direction, and received wrong thoughts from thoughts or wrong people.

The word, free will; has a clear seductive understanding. Never underestimate the word free will.

It is only limited to life or death—eternal life with what is right.

Or eternal death without what is right.

God Almighty's Love is Agape. Agape is «despite every-
thing."
Don't miss the goal; that is the same as Sin. "Of sin, be-
cause they believe not on me; ..." Jesus Christ says.
And believe it is trustful faithfulness.
Welcome to freedom, Indeed.

And let these words carry you all the way to the end.

Release yourself from your snare of understanding.

And The Blessings
From
Jesus Christ.

CONTENTS

Part One

The manipulating Hero.

There was a man on a bridge, somewhere out there. Looking down in an Ocean, an abyss, to end everything. A bridge so far down that no one made able to survive. Anxiety and depression has followed him long enough to get ready.

To jump down is easy. The least I could do. One foot out, the other right after, and let gravity fix the rest. In that second in free fall, he regretted. From where do thoughts come? After it is too late, by action from thought, and this is a testimony of one who survived.

What has manipulating people to do with suicide, they are usually not suicidal. But a cause of it, and they are good at it. They don't do it. They do it because they are one with it.

Manipulate; synonyms; control, influence, use/turn to one's advantage, exploit, maneuver, engineer, steer, direct, and last, twist someone around one's little finger, and they are good at it. A fowler is good at laying a snare. To ensnare, From Strong's dictionary: Snare (metallic), also a spring net (as spread out like lamina).

Psychopathy is traditionally a personality disorder characterized by persistent antisocial behavior, impaired empathy, remorse, bold, unrestrained, and self-centered traits. The word psychopathy is joining the Greek words; psyche, soul, and pathos; suffering, feeling. (Wikipedia)

If you fear being a psychopath, you are probably not. It is no longer a diagnosis help for psychopaths, simply because they cannot accept they are one. To make sure, we are not talking of the psychopath with a long sentence in prison, but the ordinary psychopath, hidden in society. I use this term to open the eyes of the readers. I instead use the term as a manipulating hero. They are easy to like if you are one of them who is looking for someone you can look up to it, or to be related to it, and then you are in the trap. So this chapter will not be about the manipulator, but rather about those who end up in Fowlers Net.

I was watching a documentary about some scientists, which researched birds some years ago. The net they put up where placed in a very conscious place.

They consider the light. You made blinded by the lightning as to say. Where the birds usually travel. Among bushes and shrubs, where there is no open view. Like physical hindrance to seeing clearly. When the net correctly put up, it is only to have little patience, and wait. Now I got the revelation when the bird entered the net. I discover, the more, the bird was moving, the more the bird involved itself into the trap. More you progress, more trapped are you. Then Psalms 124.7-8. (Bible) Comes to my mind: Our help is in the name of the Lord, who made heaven and earth.

Basically, you can't release your self. If you think you can, you will be more trapped into it. The Fowler looks at himself as a hero, who can guide you out of your trouble in life. People avoid the net because they know how to prevent it by experience, or discernment. Or it takes one to now one, and the picture I got; they will never release you. If they release you, they find someone else, to abuse. Whatever it is. To fight with them, you will lose the battle before being trained and put on your full armor. You need two hands in the name of the Lord. Who softly release you, without breaking your wings. The scientist is not the problem here, because they "examine" you, after release you softly from the net, and set you free. It is also what Jesus Christ will do, and set you free. So do not fight the fight, you will lose until you are ready, free from the net.

Mainly in the book is about; deception. Mostly, we let us deceive, be deceived. Mainly we want to blame some-one. Find someone to accuse. But if we know what we didn't know, we wouldn't do it. Simple as that.

You are more involved in the trap than you are willing to admit. The manipulating Hero might comfort you, give you confidence, you didn't know you had. He is very good to twist around one's little finger. In Proverbs, one book in the Bible says: "Surely in vain, the net made spread in the sight of any bird." They do not see it; still, they see it. Mainly this is deception. You might have warned to stay away from these persons, which saw the manipulating Hero's net. Your senses warned you, but you ignored it.

Like an old mother of one manipulating Hero, she comes into the living room; you were sitting. With sadness in her face, and she said: "You know, my son is very ma-nipulating, and he doesn't give up before he got what he wants." Her sadness was a part of your grief, which she understands that you have involved yourself in some-thing you shouldn't. Also of what she has confirmed in her past life. These people do not spare anyone, not even their parents, and since they are Hero's in arguments, everyone will lose—even their parents. Love is also to learn to take authority. Then you can stop them before they get started.

Next step.

How to avoid getting caught.

"And by good words and fair speeches deceive the hearts of the simple." The biblical terms will follow this book. The root of the words in the Bible will be the key to this book.

Let's look;

hearts of simple; harmless; also apparently a primary word; worthless; it can also be; noisome, wicked. In dictionary even; simple; gullible, naive.

They are worthless, in that meaning, they are open for evilness, and since the hearts of simple made fooled. Thus they have not taken the trouble to work on their personality. They take everything that made said for granted. They do not seek revelation—no gift to discern. Our strength must be in Jesus Christ. Not in the understanding or doctrine of others. We will be learning to know Him better through the book. The manipulating Hero like to reign. They beguiling unstable souls. Or to entrap them as to say, and the gullible; has no real value or use. What they need is a revelation; means to expose something that which was hidden.

"; and by good words and fair speeches…" flatter so they can talk well about you. So they can attach you to themselves. With a flatter, they bless you, and not to an Almighty God or Jesus Christ, son of God.

Our surroundings characterize us because we alone are gullible. Gullible is a negatively charged word, which we must get out of it. We imagine everything.

"Do all things without murmurings and disputing," disputing means; imagination. One of Satan's fortifications is prejudice. Prejudice is narrow, arrogant, and it is destructive. In other words, foolishness. "But God hath chosen the foolish things of the world to confound the wise, and God hath chosen the weak things of the world to confound the things that mighty." To confound means to shame down or put to the blush. Be ashamed. Honor God before, man. "But God hath revealed them unto us by his Spirit; for the Spirit searcheth all things, yea, the deep things of God." To reveal the mystery of the deep things of God, you surely need God's Spirit. To show something, you have to start seeking. Start with your heart, because Almighty God sees to heart. Capture your mind, test everything. Because Devil, the accuser, hang around. He is the father of all snares, the net can be whatever, as people, Ism, religion, which usually is a sect and doctrine that comes from man's mouth, the human man's mind. Never stop asking yourself where thought's come from it. A net is set up, from which point of view you stand. The deception goes around and hang's around. It's devilish. "And this I pray, that your love may abound yet more and more in knowledge and all judgement." The knowledge has to be an acknowledgment into the truth, which made revealed from an Almighty God. A deeper understanding you never had. In all judgment, the discernment in you which made shown from Almighty God.

Psalm 91.

Plural of Christians worldwide have Psalm 91 hanging on their wall. Without having a deeper meaning, understanding of Psalm 91. If you are not in Jesus Christ, Christ will not be in you. Without revelation, it will only be a religious understanding, which is dangerous like hearts of simple; worthless.
"I will say of the Lord; He is my refuge and fortress; my God; in him, I will trust." Book of Psalms is written mostly by King David, a man of God, chosen. All books in the Bible are from men who were called by God— elected by Him. Even Solomon. Righteousness men, humble for God, and if not, they repented. They lived as they speak, and they failed but was standing. They put their words and lived it. No compromise. They fell into sin but did not live in sin. Powerfully obedient men, God was their fortress, their defense, because they walked with God. They did what they made told. To walk in the word of God, in all simplicity. They were with God, and God was with them.

"Surely He shall deliver thee from the snare of the fowler, and from the noisome pestilence." Noisome; desire; also ruin; calamity, iniquity, perverse thing, very wickedness. And pestilence; plague. You can even say Noisome people with pestilence and plague.
"Because he hath set his love upon me, therefore will I deliver him: I will set him on high because he hath known my name." And this read worthless hearts of simple Christians today. They don't walk with God, and God Almighty does not walk with them, and so it's pestilence and plague.
Love Christ, be in Him, and He will be in you. He has known my name: Known; acknowledge. Also, discern. The manipulative Hero is not always visible; he stands in the bushes. At a distance, and waiting. Fowler's net will never be big enough, for those who end up there, and the net makes them self-pity. Self-pity makes them self-righteous. Self-righteous make them stuck to the snare.

In my youth, when I was old enough to become independent. A gay friend told me, in a gay relationship, it is quite typical to bring in a third person for sexual display. In a relationship, there is no room for more than two. So here is a dominant relationship on which one wants more than he already has. In psychological writings, the psychopath has extreme sexual behavior. Controlling, authoritative, and convincing, and the manipulative Hero has a partner who looks up to him—and made convinced. They live with a noisome person who desires, are perverse, and very wicked with pestilence and plague. To open eyes in Fowler's net is not pleasant. One man can realize you from the snare without ruin your wings, Jesus Christ, the savior.

The sexual unfolding of the same sex is nothing but that; they cultivate their egocentric image, reflecting their gender, and worship of sexual ego and want something which can mirror a grandiose self-image in. Narcissism in a closet soon has to get out of it. Narcissism is sin, and self-pity is self-righteous. Self-righteousness is also sin.

An American newspaper made a while ago a ten on the top list of professions with the most psychopaths. On that list, priests, pastors, and religious leaders ended up, and come to believe that God calls many of these, we must think again.

When my wife gave birth for the second time, her husband, that is I, was present. In Norway, we have Birth-place Hotel, which the family can be with a mother and newborn child. The evening, the day after birth, we joined a community gathering of fresh parents' information. What amazed me was that midwives had to warn fathers to abstain from having sex with their wives. Something that I thought was unnecessary to provide. But it turns out that other cultures, especially Arabic, do not take his wife's attention, which must make stated. When going out into the world, multiplying and becoming many, has become a religious mark, and a submissive net for those who ended up there. There is no freedom in religion. Just a pure satisfaction for their sexuality. Especially for men, but where do you find the Fowlers net here?

From self-appointed religious leaders, who make a statement with outgoing self-confidence, with conviction. With convincing. There is an ethnic and sectarian net in every camp and every country, making room for a manipulating hero. Jesus Christ says: «And many false prophets shall rise, and shall deceive many.» Multiplied, it is pretty many. The root of the word, the false prophet, is; a religious impostor. Jesus Christ called Devil for a father of all lies, meaning he is pretty good at it. A controlling person is only interested in training others. Not themselves. A manipulating attitude. Hypocrisy; is an actor under an assumed character.

But let's talk about laziness, which makes us lazy when we can't stand to get up in the morning. When the thought tells me I'm tired. What to do, when taking short cuts. Path of ease. Laziness is the same as the delay, which I am good at it. To be slow. A lazy servant earns nothing—a lazy person. Who has not fed birds, and some of them are more daring than others. Murphy's law, what can happen, will happen. It is not boldness, but laziness.

Take chances without being in control of everything you do. You will become manipulated to end up into the net, sooner or later. Take control before others do, and that is hard work. Fear and laziness; Jesus calls them wicked. Building your house on the rock is a lot of work. Do not murmur, and try to control your mind. Trusting God Almighty, without doing His will, is laziness.

What does anger do to our minds? What is the cause of it? When you heat a casserole, and it starts to boil. It needs Energy. Where does Energy come from it? Energy needs to have a source, and something to lead it through. Cut off the source, no Energy, no heat. Simple answer, and do not entertain it. I went into my angry thoughts, and I saw it was boiling, active. Turn off the switch im-mediately, and break the source. Anger in Fowler's net, wrap you more into it. Control your mind—self-con-trolled, sharp in a thing. We can't accuse the accuser with anger. Then he finds your error and attacks you, and put you down. Devil means accuser. So you can't blame the accuser simply because the accuser knows that your flesh is weak—an easy target. Humbleness is to have self-control. If doubt, you end up in nowhere. I did. Even I believe it is no doubt in faith. Strengthen yourself and believe. Our help is in the name of the Lord.

Frustrations, what is that, anger? Not so sure about that, let us see. Disappointment is contrary to salvation, which puts you in a trap. Salvation means; to set free. Frustrations are to know the salvation, and you can not do anything about it. Anger is concrete. Frustration is a temper but no idea of what to say or what to do. Frustration is silly and lost the opportunity to have any control over the situation, a fool. He comes with slander; a fool lay open his folly. He who trusts in his own heart is a fool—one who acts obstinate. Fool denotes, first and foremost, one who is morally and religiously a fool. His anticipation has its origin from the heart as well as from the head. His spiritual depravity hampers the use of the abilities and powers he has made granted—thereof frustration. Frustrations do not turn on earthquake measurements, but slightly disturbing to radio signals. It creates unrest, at the same time, without being noticed but only itself. Frustrated people can be good at hiding. What should emerge today? When it finally comes, it comes in anger and remorse. Therefore, frustrations are made hidden as much as possible. Frustrations are a terrible atmosphere. You can sense it on your body, and an annoyance. Then we have concluded: Frustrations connected to anger, remorse.

Everything dies once, fools, and other people, and on the journey, the emotions come along. Knowing the true salvation is what few have done, and if they have experienced it, revealed the salvation, there are even less who can complete the race. To work on his salvation is tiring, the lazy one will say, he who is resting in faith, where it's just a matter of when they will end up in the net.

We like Heros, who does "save the world" and do things that other people cannot do. Heros look is alike good. Even they swear, kill, and fool around with women. Before I always loved Hero, as a daydreamer, I made lost in my fantasy world.
In our time, we live in a standstill between fiction and reality. Turned the ear away from the truth, to fables and what itches in our ear. Hearing, sight, and mouth are connected, and it's usually pleasant when all three are in function or put into the right position. The Bible made written in simplicity that no one today made able to understand. It is one truth beyond everything but we slightly get manipulated by Heros, which itches someone's ear. Heros you find everywhere, in Hollywood, Olympic arena, among Religions and Politics, to mention some.

A hero does not necessarily become a person or thing I already say; what about Culture, which is very manipulating. I once read a book called Culture-shock. The shock when two cultures meet and the total misunderstanding they can have. But here comes a revelation, all Culture is a trap for those who live into it. How did they get there? By birth, family, and structure of the country, they live in it. They make made up of the Human Mind.

14

It is for order and control. Control to keep them continues in the trap, to make sure they don't get out of there.

In India's culture contains a religion called Hinduism,
which means they burned their wives before their husbands died, in old time, before human rights. After World
War II they have to stop burning their wives. Instead,
they just thrown out. Because the reason for being a
widow after their husbands died, they convinced that the
widows had lived foolish lives, or outside the framework
provided in their previous life, before this. So today, the
family's thrown the widow out into the streets instead.
Welcome to the culture trap. Culture is hard to admit;
they live it, a manipulating Hero.
How can the bird get out of this? From the Lord, who
made heaven and earth! In every sentence in this book,
there is an answer; you have to start looking. Then it will
be opened for you, or out of a snare.

To Discern.

After telling them a parable, Jesus Christ said to His disciples a similitude, fictitious, to liken: «That seeing they
may see, and not perceive, and hearing they may hear,
and not understand…». Perceive; to discern clearly; to
know; be aware; consider knowledge; appear discernment the ability to judge well. It is a perfect draft to dis-

cern. The dissertation is necessary to resist everything, and everyone.

«Prove all Things; hold fast that which is good.» The word Prove; to test, literally or figuratively; to discern, examine. Discern is to perceive or recognize. Discernment comes after the ability to see.

Harmony is part of the word; peace, but without discerning, it is deceiving.

Why?

A person was visiting a family. He invited in. With good food and pleasant conversation, he thanks for the hospitality, and to everyone he meets, he puts pressure on how harmonious and enjoyable it was. After that, another enters the same house, and he only discerns, control, falsity, and backtalk. In the "pure," he perceives impurity. We come no way without discernment. A net will always make spun. Be aware. I've seen how other people bound people. Physically and mentally. No freedom. They think so and live in a harmonious glare, with no ability to discern without judging.

When Adolf Hitler, the leader of Germany, came to power in 1933. He was the man who would lift Germany after the defeat after the First World War. The originator of World War II, and he did it miraculously. Finally, the German people got one they could look up to it. Then the symptoms began to register, and if you are enamored, you will be blind. Hitler's: "Rise and Fall"

became a reality. But those with judgment took his hat and left the country. Before, it was too late.
It has been said: "It is not the dictator who is a threat, but the people." Learn how to discern-getting to know people. The way they walk, the way they talk. Human being, know them in the hallway. Not a human fear. It's just an obstacle to see, clear. There are people with a hidden agenda, and it can be yours.

How many parents have not warned their daughters? Against marrying someone, they are in love. One who has everything it needs to be manipulative. The objective made set aside. They just want a king with a head taller, to regret the rest of her life it will come later. They are losing judgment in favor of emotions, and emotions are unable to hold onto the good. Feelings are not freedom, but a big trap.
« …those by reason of use have their senses exercised to discern both good and evil.»

I just love the story of King David. Before he became King. King Saul vs David. When the chosen people of Israel got the promised land God Almighty appoint judges and prophets to lead the land of Israel. Inserted with the Spirit of God, they were advocates of God Almighty. Obedient men who obeyed. A prophet means; a foreteller; an inspired speaker; a poet; Prophet.

They had a living relationship with a living God, and they did His will, mostly. God is eternal. It is not the will of the people. Over time, rebelliousness is a fact. The last judge just got to know it on his body, Samuel, chosen by God Almighty, spoke on behalf of God. Not from himself. His sons did not, then the fatal happens. The people want a king, not a judge. They want what the world have. Almighty God said to Samuel: »Hearken unto the voice of the people in all that they say unto thee: for they have not rejected thee, but they have rejected me, that I should not reign over them.» Hearken; a primitive root; to hear intelligently; obedience, discern.

Meaning: Discern unto their voice.

Samuel said to the people earlier, when they had opened up to worship idols: «If ye do return unto the Lord with all your hearts, then put away the strange gods and Ashtaroth from among you, and prepare your hearts unto the Lord, and serve Him only, and He will deliver you out of the hand of the Philistines.»

They did as He said, but when hearts are not wholly with Him, they do not endure to the end. Man wants something to relate to it. Their choices fade to themselves, often, with consequences. A manipulative hero one they could look up to it. A human being can become an idol for humans, according to circumstances, they chose a king. God obeyed the people because God discerned their hearts, they found a man, after the hearts of the people, a man, young and beautiful. There was not a man

among the children of the people who were more beautiful than him. He was a head taller than all the people.
One, they could look up to it. One they could relate to it.
His name was Saul. Saul was of the tribe of disobedient
Benjaminites. Rebellion can be inherited.
Samuel anointed Saul. To the King, and the people got
what they wanted, but rejected the Almighty God. With
the Spirit of the Lord, the Holy Spirit, the Spirit of a living God came upon Saul. Here, the seduction becomes
complete because God wants to show people that it is
only God's hand that they can be redeemed. Of the
Fowlers net, and to relate alone to an Almighty God.
With all their hearts.
To be subjugated by a king, a disobedient, with their own
choices, and the consequences of the choices they make.
A king of oppression take the best of it all. Under a kingdom where everything was once of God, finally becomes
a human being. Therefore Samuel, inspired by God, says
to Saul:»…Behold, to obey is better than sacrifice, and to
hearken than the fat of rams».
It is so that a spider spins its web for its benefit. My
opinion is when a human being becomes more like a
human than obedience to an Almighty God. It becomes
an animal. Remember, «The Fall of Man» is not a concept but a fact, and Saul is seen as rebellious, stubborn,
and self-righteous. Did what suited him under the circumstances, and not under an Almighty God. But the
people got a king, he could choose from the best, of all.

Thus, confidence in Saul disappeared, and he had to spin his net, to maintain his royal power. David made chosen, small but big enough to fight the enemy. David was not avenged; it was Saul. A prosecutor of rank.

Some accused based on the circumstances. Others have the discernment to "prove all things and hold fast that which is good." If you cannot discern, you will accuse, assume before relevant facts. Saul did it on several occasions. Who has not been judges with their assumptions? David was fearless but also fair. He had an honest heart according to the will of God Almighty, and if he did wrong, it was repentance. David loved Saul but never ended up in Saul's net. The way the people did. So David was persecuted by Saul. God Almighty, and those with a whole heart before the Lord, not look at what man is looking at: The people. For they look on the outside, for they cannot discern. At the same time, the Lord is looking to the heart, and those who are complete with the Lord can discern a human being. They recognize falsehood and injustice. They do not want what people want but do the will of God Almighty, with disobedience, the Spirit of the Lord departed from Saul, and the Spirit of the Lord came upon David that day.

The right man in the right place with a heart for the Almighty. David walked in the name of the Lord, not in his power. Therefore he did not end up in Saul's net but he loved Saul, with a heart from the heart of God Almighty. Vengeance does not lead to anything.

The story of David before he became King shows us that Saul persecuted him. Remember this: Saul repented with his lips, time after time, disobeying but he never regretted it with his heart, and it was Samuel the Prophet who was inspired by God.

Saul is, to be a perfect manipulative picture, how manipulative people are, and the people were fooled. With one, they could look up to it but David had discernment, and he was a warrior. One with authority because he was fearless, and no one needed to look up to it. When the hatred in Saul took over, David loved the enemy. He responded with the right action. Even when he could kill Saul, he only cut off a flick of his robe in a cave, when all circumstances made it possible. Because as David said: "Let the Lord judge between you and me, and let the Lord avenge me on you. But my hand shall not be against you. As the proverb of the ancients says: "Wickedness proceeds from the wicked". But my hands shall not be against you."

He made himself small in Saul's eyes. No self-righteous judge. Vengeance belongs to the Lord. Saul's assumptions against David had consequences for Saul. David discerned and held on to the good. The Bible says, "There is no one righteous. Not one." That's because everyone falls no one is without sin. Therefore, we must forgive so that Heavenly Father can forgive us. Unforgiveness is a snare. Forgiveness is wonderful. Thus, David was of the Heart of God. David hated injustice against Almighty God, so he killed Goliath, who mocked his God. In the beginning, Saul did God's will until it no longer suited him.

David kept God to the end. "Endure to the end, and you shall be saved." The root of the word saved; means to get rid of it. Obvious this was to David. God Almighty chose Saul but pride took over and ended his own life. God wanted Saul to show His people the consequences of having a king. David was elected King to show the people that one must have a whole heart for the Lord. A people bound by their own will, a rebellious people, they just wanted a king, and not one inspired by God. David lamented Saul and his sons after being persecuted for almost 17 years. King David took care of God's Spirit, which came upon him when God Almighty anointed him. "Quench not the Spirit." It came entirely over David with Saul fresh in memory.

Some time ago, on a mission field. I found a path, a gentle way, to seek the Lord Jesus Christ. On the way in front of me, a vision, I saw a fog cloud. In the fog, blurred, I saw Jesus Christ. He stood there sad, accused by the scribes and the Pharisees. With the high priest above him with false accusations. Mocked and spitting on, but up in all this, I saw Jesus with meekness. The meekness does not strike back. Meekness; humble; gentle; mild. Also pain. Pain over the injustice they did. The Pharisees were never able to accept the truth, like Saul.

They made convinced that they had it, their power structure raised them even above Jesus Christ. In the fog where everything was blurred I saw it clearly, the wrong they did. Their self-righteousness had seduced them, and a total lack of humility. On the cross, after the charges and sentenced to death. Then Jesus said, "Forgive them for they do not know what they are doing." No self-defense. Among the high priest, the Pharisees, Jesus Christ chooses to be silent, like a slaughtered lamb. He opened his mouth only to confirm the truth to overcome the manipulative forces. Jesus Christ stands rooted and grieved. Among the Pharisees, those he called hypocrites, during the time he walked among the Israeli people.

«Woe unto you, scribes and Pharisees, hypocrites! For ye are like unto whited sepulchers, which indeed appear beautiful outward, but are within full of dead men's bones, and of all uncleanness».

The root of the word; hypocrite; is; an actor under an assumed character.

To put it this way; they were beautiful to look at, and someone to look up to it. Only those who can discern can see the bones of death and all kinds of impurities.

When Jesus spoke to the people and his disciples about the scribes and Pharisees, he brought forth the manipulative hypocrisy of them in an excellent way. They rose above all others, lesser the people with heavy burdens, even they will not touch them with a finger. They liked to be seen by people. They would like to have the seats of honor, and they are first seats in the synagogues. They exalted themselves. The Pharisee hypocrites ate up a widow's house. Even their mother, they can exploit—the heroes of manipulation. Everything seems to be okay with their whitewashed walls. But Jesus Christ took authority over them. Jesus called them blind guides because they didn't see the light, Jesus was. We must have light to see. The scribes and Pharisees themselves were righteous and proud. They used their net to catch children to teach them, and made them worse than themselves. A philosopher said, "Give me a little child, and I can make it whatever you want." So will the manipulative Hero. He never gives up. They had no light on anything other than their own opinion. On the outside, they were righteous to the people a power elite. Like a manipulative hero. They honored God with their lips, and not with all their heart. The Pharisee can be found in all walks of life today. From the Director to the theological, to the religious.

Jesus opened the eyes of the people. He wants to teach us to discern, to see all kinds of impurities, and to hold fast that which is good. To judge the ability to distinguish between both good and evil. To discern is the whole pillar, foundation. Something everyone has, but they haven't exercised their senses. Without the applied ability to discern, we made trapped in something or someone.

God Almighty created all things according to its kind. What did He create? Elements? There are fundamental elements in all created things. Early-stage in all fetuses; animals, humans. Then they are similar, but after growth and development. They become an animal, according to their kind, and mankind created according to God likeness, in His Image. Thus the necessary elements adapted to each species. When something is similar, they are not necessarily the same. Jesus Christ used parables to describe the kingdom of God. He gave us pictures in description. Not everyone took it. "That seeing they may see, and not perceive." But with an open heart, disciples in all simplicity, they got it visible. Responsive souls, with discernment. Disciples; a learner; pupil. Also follower. One who learns to discern. From a gift that made given. To all. To discern is not an intellectual understanding, then you will be deceived. But Spiritually to observe what is good, or evil. Who do you want to be a follower of it? Who do you want to be like it? A question mark can cause you confusion.

Take a stand, stick to it, to confusion.

 To distinguish between a Prophet and a manipulative hero, then you must discern. You must get to know Him —He who releases you from the snare. A Prophet has authority; so can the manipulative. They convince; that God Almighty inspires the Prophet by God Almighty. The manipulator is inspired by itself. The wheat and the tar grow together exactly alike, until the grain gets grain

on it and can show off the true, but the weeds of confusion. The bearded darne-klinten is very similar to the
wheat until maturity reveals its true nature.

Confusion.

When two magnetic counterpoints meet, they bump
apart. The bright day cannot wander with the night.
Dawn of the light, it's a battle until the day dominates.
And vice versa. Everything in this world has a counter-
part. In the world of flavors, flavors can blend, and give
a hot tasting experience. Who hasn't tasted anything that
looks delicious? But it didn't taste good, or not according
to expectations. The closest thing you can call confusion,
disorder. "For God is not the author of confusion, but of
peace ...". Confusion; instability; disorder; unstable. The
Greek word "actustasia" means as much confusion, as a
disorder. Where there is confusion, there is the disorder.
Confusion is an imbalance, its instability. Suppose we
not exercised to discern, both good and evil, will there be
confusion and disorder—an instability.

"A double-minded man is unstable in all his ways."
Double-minded, vacillating, confused between both good
and evil. Everything as a Christian born again; I did with
peace, seemed right. Without peace, it ended up in error
or failure. Peaceful when we have a relationship with the
Lord Almighty. A mess of confusion and disorder when

we are unstable and lost balance, peace is to join divine prosperity; rest in Him—Almighty Father in heaven. Father in heaven sent His son Jesus Christ as a rescue team for this lost world. But with deceiving, they get confused, and disorder is a fact.

There is more or less corruption in developing countries, which is not corruption, other than confusion, and corrupted hearts. It can be Culture or religion, Isms. Oppression of the people, control. One leans on what others do then to search into the core of what is right. Then confusion becomes a fact. Confusion is a lie told many times until it is accepted as a truth. It is where the disorder comes in. The structure of complexity is corrupt hearts, unclean hearts, bad ideas.

«But those things which proceed out of the mouth come forth from the heart, and they defile the man.» Defile; to make profane:- Call common, pollute, unclean.

Without honesty, no one comes out of it. Other than getting into a mess chaos no one made able to see. God Almighty created the cosmos into an order. The disorder is chaos—rebellion against Creator and creation. Don't think you're innocent, there are very few that are, none by fact.

Jesus Christ made sentenced to death without sin. He was rooted in what God the Father had sent him to here on Earth.

Unbelief is rooted in disobedience and complete confusion. Unbelief is defective, something everyone wants, a rebellion against the Creator. Anything that offends will one day made removed. The Greek word offended, classical Greek; skandalon; offending, seduction: A snare to temptation; English; scandalize; scandal; stumbling blocks. Jesus' parable of the wheat and tares tells us how easy it is to be deceive.

The nature of confusion and disorder must be:» Prove all things; hold fast that which is good.»

Unbelief is corruption, and corruption is ordinary like the tares. The answer to the redemption lies between the lines, for revelation. We believe in an Almighty God beyond everything. What are we doing in the middle of it? In confusion, and acknowledge on it, is the worst part, then humility; is calling. The pride stand against it.

The opposite pole of magnetism in both good and evil. It comes more in the name of redemption, "A man in God's image, according to His likeness." God created the cosmos and everything in it, in order, and in His image and His picture, we can start with something great.

Forgiveness.

Forgiveness is wonderful.
Forgiveness is for you. A relationship with the Lord Almighty.

But some people act like unforgiveness is a punishment for those who are trespasses. "But if you do not forgive their trespasses, neither will your Father forgive your trespasses." Read this: "Jesus Christ has made it ready for us, receive today. He gave His life for us.

 You think your life is miserable. Instead, think about what Jesus did for you. His life is unconditional; whole Hearted. Pure Love. He who got accused by Religious leaders at His time. Whipped and beaten, to the blood, sentenced to death. Mocking and spitting on. He had to walk on the street up to Calvary. Where Christ had crucified for us. Gave His life, overcame death, He rose again on the third day, by Father in heaven, and made it possible for us to have a new life.

I have seen how people have "fought for their rights." Before they know it, they became self-righteous, and the bitter root in their faces. Have a relationship with forgiveness instead. Be in me, Jesus Christ says, and I will be in you. Pride is arrogant-a lack of humbleness. Knowledge is proud, and your acknowledgment will make you stuck there. It is no way out. My favorite quote: "All I know is that I know nothing." It can be a paradox. If one is righteous, he lives it.
Suppose anyone tells everyone that he is righteous, he just became self-righteous. Word can be a trap, so we can be. It is the essence of forgiveness. It has to made built

on rock, from inside. The unclean is coming from within, Jesus Christ said. The same does the clean.

«But I say unto you, Love your enemies, bless them that curse you, do good to them that hate you, and pray for them which despitefully use you, and persecute you:..». Jesus Christ lived what he said. When you can discern, you are also able to take authority. If not, your mouth must be made sealed, and the power must be visible. Everything Jesus Christ said, was from His Heavenly Father. Jesus took authority over leadership and even un-righteous people, and at the same time He forgive them for their transgressions.

My story of being manipulated would be a dead-end without forgiveness. But also the ability to rest in this: "Vengeance is mine, says the Lord." It is the first step to being set free from Fowler's net. The second is to have a relationship with Him.

«Blessed be the Lord, who hath not given us a prey to their teeth.» The best part is: When you get released from it. But this is important, don't make your story in your favor. You will lose. Make yourself a Helper-right-eous one, and can judge. It is demanding. How can we take authority and, at the same time, put everything in His Hands?

To know what is right or wrong, ability to make the right decisions, with substance and confidence. The knowl-edge that an Almighty God is with you all the way.

30

«Now Faith is the substance of things hoped for, the evidence of things not seen.» Faith; a primary verb; to convince; assurance; but most important; to make a friend. Friendship with an Almighty God. Peace with Him, not necessarily the world. He is a living God, not a religion.

I trusted everybody until the opposite is proven. That can be a failure. Prove everything, and hold fast to what is right. It should be the basement against all manipulating Hero's.
When God Almighty said, in the beginning: «Let there be Light,» He divided the light from the darkness for us to see clearly. «…by the word of God, so things which are seen were not made of things which do appear». Which do appear; means also; to lighten, be seen, shine. Jesus Christ is the Light. Which we do, when we let Him appear. He can divide the light from the darkness. Do not doubt, but have Faith—Trustfully in Him. Everybody who wants to be in the Light will become visible like forgiveness. In the net, it only contains the Fowler's opinion. Be released. Free as a bird. Like it was in the beginning of creation.

Part Two

Depression and Anxiety.

When the melancholy comes over you, a global sadness, you can not touch and feel—climate change in you. Then depression and Anxiety are just around the corner. In the Book of Ecclesiastes (Bible), King Solomon says, Vanity of vanities. Vanity of vanities, all is Vanity.
 Also meaning: Emptiness.
For me, King Solomon struggle with Anxiety. Melancholy and emptiness (Vanity), the foundation for all depression and Anxiety. It is from depression and Anxiety: Where do all the thoughts come from it? Comes into its place, Suicidal thoughts. Which makes you do, what you should not do!

There was a man on a bridge, somewhere out there. Looking down in an Ocean, an abyss, to end everything. A bridge so far down that no one made able to survive. Anxiety and depression have followed him long enough to get ready.

To jump down is easy. The least he could do. One foot out, the other right after, and let gravity fix the rest. In that second, in free fall, he regretted. Where do thoughts come? After it is too late. By action from thought. This is a testimony of one who survived.

In the service of depression, it's not much to say. It made not ordered in the chaos. To put thought into action, demands courage, or lack of it; discourage, and it is those who "Just do it!"

To think differently, doesn't help. Can you bend a thought, like a verb in a grammar? Can you close your mind for thoughts? Is there any error in humanity's understanding, any room or space to move thoughts into something? Or is there someone beyond everything? Do not despair; it is easy to say.

We were "free" as the bird to fly.
Then we were caught by something.

Our soul has escaped as a bird from the
the snare of the fowlers: The snare is broken, and we have survived.
Our help is in the name of the Lord. Who made heaven and earth.

The devil is the opposite of God Almighty. The Greek word for devil is; Diabolos, which means: Accuser, one who splits, evil speaker and accusations, one that confuses. Jesus Christ calls him the father of all lies. The author of all lies.

Jesus Christ said: «Come to Me, all you who labor and are heavy laden, and I will give you rest.»
How about discouragement; best way to get out of Anxiety, is to get to know it. For God has not given us a spirit of fear, but of power and a sound mind.
My testimony I will lay down. But it takes one to know one.

If the unhealthy darkness in you is the light, then can you imagine how dark, darkness is.

The lamp of the body is the eye. If therefore your eye is good,
your whole body will be full of light.
But if your eye is bad (unhealthy), your whole
body will be full of darkness. If therefore the light that is in you is darkness, how great is that darkness!

I had two choices when I needed help: Psychiatry or Jesus Christ. I chose Jesus Christ. Because I look at Jesus Christ as a person, He was my redemption. Jesus says: The Spirit of the Lord is upon Me because he has anointed Me to preach the gospel to the poor. He has sent Me to heal the brokenhearted, to proclaim liberty to the captives, and recovery of sight to the blind. To set at liberty,

those who are oppressed: To proclaim the acceptable
year of the Lord.

Take My yoke upon you and learn from Me, says Jesus
Christ,
for I am gentle and lowly in heart, and you will find rest
for your
souls, For My yoke, is easy, and My burden is light.

Jesus Christ is the liberator and the redeemer. Never give
up. There is hope because it is life after dark.

Let not your heart be troubled; you believe in God,
also, believe in Me.
I am the Way, the Truth and the Life, "says Jesus Christ.

Jesus Christ is the light in the dark:
In Him was life, and the life was the light of men.
And the light shines in the darkness and the darkness, did
not comprehend it.

Darkness always stands against the light.
In light, there are colors.
In the light, it is Faith.
In light, there is Hope.
In the light, it is Love.

Have anyone experience sitting on the subway, and felt like someone tries to strangle you with a transparent plastic bag - you might experience Anxiety.

It feels like everyone watching. You try to find a place to put your eyes, and likely you want to walk off the subway at the next station. You can't grab Anxiety, like a spider. It is like a melancholy—a sadness that is not rooted in anything. Anxiety is the same. Where did this started, and when? Are depression and Anxiety basically from sin? Is it spiritual? The psychiatrist will rip his hair of if someone asks a question like that. But let us start from the beginning.

An ordinary life, grow up with a single mother, divorced, in the seventies. The great decade, for some, when school was not favorite, and humbleness was not a part of my grammar. More rebellious, like the "great" seventies, when I was old enough. Independent, but not mature. I got a job after education; and said to myself: I am on my one now, let's experience life, and live it. Realize yourself, and "just do it." Been there, done that. Until emptiness takes you, after experience "everything," and "nothing" left, and you and Solomon are suddenly two of a kind.

Depression has many flavors and colors, but end up in the same. Fowler's anxiety is a net, and if you try to get out of it, you will wrap your self more into it. You are starting to have a little picture now: Thought running in your mind. Where do the thoughts come from it? Why is it proven that Anxiety is more common among them who have more than they need? To struggle in life with lack of something, a job, economy, lake of food, maybe trouble in the marriage, family, sadness which last in a period. That is in good and evil days, which most of us come over, overcome. It is part of life; everyone can handle it unless you are a narcissist, or proudness which has lost their "face." Or you have lost someone or something, and never come over it. Open your eyes, and you will see, Jesus Christ said to a blind. He saw people blurred, like trees, then everything comes true, and he could see, awesome. Anxiety blinding our minds. So we cannot see. It is dark, it is no love, joy, and peace. No hope for those who made soaked into it, but they hang out. Some learn to live with it, sadly, but true.

Diagnosis is from a human understanding and insight. Founded on the knowledge you have in the time you live in it, not on divine wisdom. A human knowledge level, understanding beyond that comes first when we seek an Almighty God. In diagnosis you can find symptoms, but it will not release completely.
Anxiety; The Titanic did not sink based on the top of the visible iceberg, but what made hidden.

In the seventies, the beginning of the eighties was the murder case in Norway, in which a man became guilty.

He got a long sentence. After serving almost the entire sentence, someone took up the murder case, with new evidence. The incident came up again, and he made acquitted on all points. He got out of prison. The case received a lot of attention. When he leaves the trial, a reporter asks: How do you feel now? He answered very calmly: It's like a swan gracefully, but the feet under below desperately paddle. Sometime you can't tell what people feel. Jesus Christ says: Come to me all of you who have a heavy burden, and I will give you rest. The word rest, a primary verb, comes to an end.

At the end of the nineties, when my Anxiety was worse, I came across a Bible verse that was very redeeming for me, or the beginning of redemption. Having tried to read books about depression and Anxiety. Contemporary books as to say.
"For God hath not given us the spirit of fear, but of power, and love, and a sound mind."
I rested in the word; a spirit of fear; spirit; a primary word; breathe hard, breeze; blow; a current of air, a spirit, an angel, demon. It was more than a diagnosis. And fear; from deos; dread; timid, faithless; fearful. So fear is a spirit and a dreadful one. Dread; synonyms: Fear, Anxiety.
 Then my head was filled with more than necessary, the spirit of discouragement. It will be a psychologically oriented versus Christ in man.

Let us go back to Solomon, a man with seven hundred wives, and a lot of concubines, who worship idols. By far the world's richest man in his present time. A broken man, disobedient to God, who received wisdom from God. Disobedient create anxiety.

With his knowledge, he uses the word like; «a broken spirit; wounded spirit; and; if thou faint in the day of an adversary, thy strength is small.»

If Solomon would live today, he had the diagnoses: Anxiety.

How to separate the tares from the wheat, when tares look alike? Let them both grow together until the harvest.

Melancholy.

At a bar sometime in the 1990s, I went for some beers after working hours, unshaven, and no plans. Just spend time with me as the only company. With a melancholy mood, which I liked. Not a sadness within me, but an outward sadness to the people around me. Being in a sphere where you see things others do not understand. At the same time, others enjoyed together with their friends. I saw a meaningless the other failed to see. There was a completely different atmosphere with me than with them. The strangest of all, I liked that atmosphere, nor was it a pity on myself. Instead, a windless sphere of melancholy.

A peculiar mood in a strange bubble. Something I tried to explain to two women who sat down gradually, which they did not recognize, and far from their world, and something I should not mention. Sometimes it is wise to let it be. To get out of it or getting into it, without a door, that is melancholy. Melancholy can be sweet in the beginning.

In my early youth, we had Pink Floyd, Bob Dylan, and many others with rebel music. Rebels ready to take over the world. Today they sing the big sad love song, which is so melancholy and narcissistic that even musclemen want to jump out of a bridge—the melancholy killer, and if you survive, you become self-pity with a grandiose self-image. Everything starts with something like the flu. Someone sneezes at you, and you got cold, and emptiness is not a medicine, just a gap. Melancholy and emptiness are in a family, thick as blood. Strongest there is.

In emptiness and vanity, you find self-pity and a place where it is accessible to made led astray since it's big. In emptiness and vanity, one finds selfishness, pride, arrogance. Emptiness is a gap, useless and takes up a lot of space. A void is something else; it is located in the air, in the sea, in the universe; cosmos. But the void is not void, since everything has elements in it. In space, most are empty but filled with elements. Everything is emptiness and vanity. In one parable Jesus Christ say's: When unclean spirits made gone out of a man, he walked through

places, seeking rest, and findeth none. Then he saith, I will return into my house from whence I come out, he findeth it empty, swept and put in order.
In emptiness, it can quickly occupy. In vain, you find arrogant, narcissistic, and love themself in a grandiose picture. Emptiness can quickly fill thoughts, which led us astray. Melancholy kills slowly. Set up a sign in front of your house: Beware melancholy, it bites.

If everyone had the same disease; melancholy; then no one would have declared themselves ill, and no one would ask themselves: What is melancholy, and where does it come from? What if the melancholy says to himself, as he walks through places, seeking rest, and finds none ?: "I will return to a house where it is empty, swept and put in order." What then?

In Norway, it is a fact that more people die from suicide than in traffic. But what can we do? The world is full of information. Informative. Diagnoses. Treatment. Why do we fall short on depression and Anxiety? The answer should be simple. First, you open up for something. Then take it home. To anyone who has taken housing, choose to stay. What decides to stay? Let's say it's a person. The person has occupied the residence us.

In Norway, in the eighty-nineties, we could hear about housing occupants. They held another man's home, and they demanded their right. They weren't interested in anyone's opinions; they just claimed it, the home. Building, Anxiety is the same. Then the Anxiety must be a person personified and intuitively controlled. What made it done? Either they occupied the occupants until it was vacant, tidy and empty. They tore down the building, or they agreed to let them stay. They learned to live with the situation, so to speak. Spiders are spinning nets, where it is possible to catch something or someone. The spider has a mission, similar to Anxiety. Anxiety does not die; it just moves on. They are looking for someone who can take housing. A house occupant, with an awareness that it is a person.

To set people free requires more than one human being. The physical body human. In this scientific world, where the body can be replaced, from anything defective. Except for the brain as a whole. This science has escalated over the last hundred years, and it will continue to do so. What about psychiatry? With educational conversation and medical "lobotomy," I chose Jesus Christ instead. With the hope of faith, with locking to release. The day I felt the Anxiety ran out of me. The day I could see a human being in my eyes again, and raise my head to an Almighty God. Creation's humiliating attitude towards an Almighty Creator. Take a slice of an apple and feel the taste. Nothing happens until you try.

A well-known politician in Norway once said in a TV interview about his Anxiety: "Anxiety is Hell." This was told of a man who had no close relationship with a God. For me, he hit the nail on the head. Anxiety is the absence of the good; love, peace; light. Anxiety is an emotion; some would say. No, I'd say it's a person. You can separate me from the Anxiety. Why? For the simple reason that I don't want it. When an individual does not wish Anxiety, they cannot possibly be one. It is only when an individual has accepted the Anxiety that they become one. A marriage: This called to yoke with someone.

Have you ever seen two big bulls, with a yoke on each neck? One follows where the other goes, not of free will, but with an acceptance. Letting go is not free will. Depression is thoughts and feelings, thoughts to open doors. For the Anxiety, then the Anxiety takes over, and make the home their own. Depression is rarely or never fun. Just convincing, to open the door for the Anxiety. The thoughts of depression and the Anxiety, they cooperate.

We have not given "Spirit of fear," but power, love, and a sound mind. In my Norwegian Bible, the "Spirit of discouragement" is used. For those with Anxiety or have had, it is a revelation in itself. Synonyms for discouragement include; depress, then everything gets bigger. The understanding of being small is only gained when you suffer from the occupation of Anxiety.

It is starting to take shape. A shape must slowly make formed like the potter make a tub, or vessel. Anxiety cannot make addressed. Invisible, but still there.

I followed a TV series when young; It's called: The Invisible Man. He became invisible under unfortunate circumstances. To become visible, they had to give him an identity. Make that mask look like his own face—gloves, clothes, and shoes to hide his invisibility. On assignment, with his invisible, he could move into areas where he should not make seen. Occasionally they discovered him, among other things, with someone throwing powder at him. Suppose they were conscious of his existence. In this way, he was made visible. To make visible something, one cannot requires understanding, especially when a person does not want to be made visible. Then I ask myself: How to make visible the invisible? Make yourself a person! Based on the personality you recognize. Make a face, put on his clothes and shoes, and yeah, you have a person. Now there is something concrete. One, you can grab something to relate. Suddenly the situation changes. Same procedure as if it were a manipulative human being. Let them manifest stand out from the dark side. To find the solution, we need to get the factors out. Call it problem ethics. Nothing is impossible for God. But the enlightenment is for you, not the Almighty God, for awareness and understanding.

God can set you free, only you lay still. The web has tangled, backlash. To loosen up, which has made tangled, requires understanding, and consciousness.

When I read knowledge books about depression and Anxiety, it didn't help much, physically, and mentally. But they gave me a greater understanding. Made the invisible visible to me. With consciousness, I could face the Anxiety in a completely different way. The depression also, for that matter.
Take, for example; they are similar to some bird species. They make nests in the tree. They are laying eggs, lay on the eggs, and keep it warm. They are nurturing their kids. Thoughts do the same, in the end, they are many, and they weigh you down.
"…and bringing into captivity every thought to the obedience of Christ…".
Capture thought buildings under obedience, Jesus Christ is the light. There you will find love and joy again, and you will love Him. Get ready to be free, don't doubt, but have faith. Faith also means; full confidence.
Or go back to psychiatry, with educational conversation. Ergo Bike. Long walks in woods and fields, with reflection on how you feel, and prescriptions with medical balance. Who says to himself: "I'm fine" many enough times until you believe it. It is also a conviction, not to freedom. Don't doubt, but have faith.

Narcissism.

Consider this; what if you like
your picture. Your mirror.
Your independent you. Until it
became blurred.

«To cry is the nicest there is,» there was one in a play
that said. Crying has the full spectrum, from deep grief
to narcissistic crocodile tears. Just as the melancholy
took off and the sadness opened up for Anxiety, when
you think that you are the only one who will die. Away
from everything. Like when I sought a congregation for
comfort. I was in a "think pity of my self mode" until the
pastor interviewed a blind young woman who had cancer
behind one eye. With a desire for life, she ascends the
podium and starts playing the piano with fingers that can
see. And there I sit and feel ashamed—a narcissistic soul,
who has nowhere to hide.

Narcissus was in Greek mythology, a beautiful young
boy in whom the nymph Echo fell in love. He did not
reciprocate her passion and is punished by the gods for
falling in love with his mirror image. To be consumed
and die; when he bent over a spring of clear water, to
quench his thirst. He became so enamored and paralyzed
by his mirror image that he died. When he died, a lily

made named after him. In the oldest myth, he went and killed himself.

Narcissus was not able to love anybody than himself. Proudness can lead to destruction.

While narcissism is an expression of the individual's behavior with the environment, the self is an expression of the individual's perception of himself. Because the concept of narcissism is related to an adverse reaction, is a narcissist more likely to be perceived as a person with the negative adjectives of narcissism, egocentric, lack of empathy, overly grand self-image, vulnerability to the offense, and so on? We explain and defend our sins. Sin can lead to depression, and our sin might find answers close up to "the truth" as a lie.

Narcissism is not anything else; they worship their egocentric mirror image that reflects their personality, worship of their ego. They want something they can reveal their grandiose self-image.
It is narcissism; in a closet, they soon have to get out of it.
Remember: Sin is Universal.
Your sin is not necessary for my sin, and the opposite.
Narcissism is about proudness, a question of honor.

Jesu Christ says: «And then many will be offended, will betray one another, and hate one another.»

Offended, from the word «scandal,» probably from a derivative: A trap-stick; snare; an occasion to fall; offense, the thing that offends, stumbling block, or entice to sin. It is nobody who hurt more than the offended, once who said, where narcissism nods consensual.

The New Testament also speaks of abuses in the meaning of what destroys the beginning faith, the weak in faith, the infirm, or unenlightened conscience. Here, misuse of Christian freedom can become an offense to others. When a stick of bait made placed in a snare, such a stick in classical Greek called; scandalize. In biblical language, this Word made used in a conveyed sense, about something that can "catch" one, a temptation.

Words can become like sourdough. "Do you not know that a little leaven leavens the whole lump."

Yeast is fermented dough, which in ancient times stored in water for later use as fermentation in the freshly made dough. Sourdough used throughout scriptures in the synagogue a picture of impurity and evil, which in this age tended to soak into everything.

Let us at least become humble. On that, we are not. Bible says: «Love endures all things.» Love; Greek Agape; charity, dear, love, to love.

48

So if love endures all things, how then can we be offended? If we experience all things! The love of the offended
is narcissism.
Like one in a play was saying: »To cry is the nicest there
is».

In Norway, when a child is unstable, it plagues other
children. Do wrong, is naughty, creates a disturbance for
everyone else. Then children's pedagogy is this; that
there must be a reason for such behavior that the child
inside is not feeling well. On that basis, they explain and
defend the child's sin, and process the child's psyche,
based on that. Based on trying to understand how the
child is feeling. Not what the child has necessarily done.
With such educational thinking, the child made caught
up in a narcissistic mindset, with an egocentric exces-
sively grandiose self-image, vulnerable to an offense,
and so on, and so on. They fall in love with their mirror
image, instead of an Almighty God beyond everything.
Everything is very well; until that day, the grandiose mirror image made blurred. That is to say, everything in
your atmosphere is shaking. Whatever it may be.
The Bible says, "Love your neighbor as yourself." It
must make based on the love of one's neighbor. This
Bible verse goes back and forth, continuously. They are
not just standing on its own, and its grandiose self-image. In this part, about Anxiety, we have a person fixed
the Anxiety. Anxiety itself is a net. But the Narcissist is

also a Fowler, with his self-pity. He receives thoughts without capturing them. In the root of the word narcissism, everything is evil, with self-righteousness and pride. Narcissism in a closet you have to get out of it.

Suicidal.

It was an early spring day, one could read in the news about a woman who had disappeared without a trace. Initially, the media speculated on something criminal had happened. Before relevant facts. Until they found her dead on the outskirts of Oslo, I don't remember all the details, but I do remember the impression it made with me. The case took a turn into a tragic event, where the woman had chosen to take her own life, and suicide became a topic in the media. I could feel it for myself, how she must have had it, desperate despair, and it didn't end. The main reason she did what she did never come out; it was never essential to me either. But watch her squirming a net she didn't come out of it. What I remember mainly were the circumstances in the period in which she made found. In Norway, we have four seasons, and spring is the one we crave most for most of us. It was a time when it was no extended winter, but neither was spring. For some of us, this is a dead and depressing period.
Strange enough, as the days get longer and brighter, everything we can look forward to is soon available.

50

The case resolved, and the only one left was my sadness. Just a week later, my feelings once again awakened. I sat in my car and notice one thing. It has come life into the trees since they are already budding. The leaves shoot forth then the summer is near. Then I felt the cry grip in me. Had she just endured? Then I saw the redemption in the spring. Spring is the beginning of life. Hope. Something to look forward to it. A redemption, I cried on her behalf: "Had she just endured." You can't always bear the sadness. That is what is the devilish thing about the melancholy. From an accuser, splitter, and father of all lies; the devil.

Then I will be reminded of December 1999, I was invited out by good friends. Celebrate an end to the last year, which is soon over. Great food at a restaurant on Oslo's pier with a good drink, and with a good mood, but at midnight I disappear quietly. Out in the night. Out in a cold starry sky. With emptiness and meaninglessness. Fresh air doesn't always do the trick. But have the opportunity to walk alone at Oslo's harbor where all the cruise ships anchor up in the summer. Now the Oslo fjord is blank and quiet. At the end of the dock, there is a raised platform where they can tether the mooring to the ship's stern.
Now the ports are empty, and the shining sea. At that moment, I decide to jump out of the platform, and out into the ice-cold fjord. But then I lift my head to the sky.

To an Almighty God, I have not yet chosen to follow. In my despair, I ask God to give me a sign, in the sky, as proof that I can jump. With one leg first, and the second leg after. Then it happens. A star shot in the middle of the sky vault right in front of me. That's when I get scared. I think I've never been so afraid ever. I frightened, in that sense, an answer to my desire. Today I know that it was God Almighty's way of preventing me from doing something I should not. Suicide is not from God but from someone who split. Thoughts can be confusion and disorder. God makes no difference to people. But he treats us differently since we are different individuals. Therefore, God Almighty, and Jesus Christ are persons and not a religion. From that day, the suicidal thoughts left me and started looking for someone out of my reach. I am very grateful for today.

Suicide can be desperate, spiritual, and last but not least, pride. Suicide is a temptation. Bible says: «There hath no temptation taken you but such as is common to man; but God is faithful, who will not suffer you to be tempted above that you are able; but will with the temptation also make a way to escape, that you may be able to bear it.» It is no easy way out. Bible also says: «…and whatsoever you shall make loosed on earth shall be loosed in heaven».
Get out of the snare. This Bible verse followed me when I struggle with Anxiety.

Suicide is when you jump, not before. This Word of God keeps me from jumping. Today I am thankful to the Father in Heaven and Jesus Christ. There is a lot of revelation about these verses that do not make it as a doctrine. "... whatsoever you shall bind on earth ..." can be answered to another Bible verse: "... and bringing into captivity every thought to the obedience of Christ ...". It is said before, and I repeat it: Where do our thoughts come from it? Whatsoever they can bind you. Release yourself from your line of thinking. How? Close your door!
«…enter into thy closet, and when thou hast shut thy door, pray to thy Father which is in secret;…»
Closet; (A spot for retirement); secret chamber.
Followers of Jesus Christ given to give life, not take any. Like Jesus Christ.

God has not given us more than we can bear. So why do people die from it?
Remember, we did not resolve until we made resolved. God's Word must reveal before we put it into action, you must make convicted of your efforts, says some. God Almighty looks to the hearts I will say. He can discern. What you have to do is not think so much. The mind has more power over you than you imagine. Then get into your closet. Close the door for thoughts, and open your mind to Jesus Christ. Jesus is Light. As God separated from darkness, and the darkness did not comprehend it.

In the dark, everything is invisible. Become visible in the Light of Christ.

Everything new is scary. Just see how horses or dogs react to something they haven't seen before, and so is it with people. Anxiety is creepy if you have not experienced it before.

Many people with Anxiety become aggressive. Emotionally aggressive. Temper. Strange enough. But that's because the senses take over. When someone says, "I don't believe it until I see it." Then they blindly trust the eye and their perception. Senses can be dominant. They made connected to a mechanical body, and make the body alive. It's called flesh.

Our flesh dominates. You almost can't think of anything else when it smells bad. Anxiety is the focus through the sensible. Anxiety has become visible. What about venting the windows on both ends. That's what you do when you pray. Closes the door and ventilates at both ends. Open your mind when enough is enough. You can open your mind. Make a decision. Now the Anxiety is manifested. Everything becomes visible during manifestation. It is not necessarily liberation but a confirmation of freedom. To deliverance. Senses what is it? They are transparent. It made download in the flesh, for joy and sorrow.

54

Emotions.

Who root canal humility?
A tooth is full of nerves. A nerve is a receiver for pain.
Pain is a sense connected to emotions. Feelings are made
connected to our brains.
The brain gives us a "hint" of pain, and it is a fraction of
a second, except for the pain that has taken root.
 The rest I leave to a dentist and his knowledge of teeth.

No one can tell me how painful it is; no one can tell me
not to trust my feelings. Nerves can be touched and felt;
I see the world from my point of view. No one is going
to tell me anything else. Lies are subjective to the subjective. Such lies are objective to the objective. The philosophy at a high level. A nerves in high tension. The pain
over a low threshold, then we unplug the connection,
then we root canal the painful humility. Humility; to turn
the other cheek. It is a pain of anxiety to hit back.
Remember: Jesus Christ loves you.

 So who root canal humility, I ask?

The feelings that power they have over us, on good and
evil. They can rule over you. They can seduce you. But
one thing I wonder, are there feelings in the kingdom of
God? God's kingdom. Of course, there is. But it is built
on a relationship to love since God is love. Love is not a

feeling. It is very present. In the kingdom of God. Fruit of the Spirit. It will flow out like metal conducting electricity. Out of it comes power. One day the light in you will become visible, and not the dark. The eye can be dominant—a sense of distinguishing light from the darkness. Remember, the blind can see, and whoever sees can become blind. It is not sensory therapy.

«Blessed are poor in spirit, for theirs is the kingdom of heaven.»

It is in all simplicity. Take captivity of your thoughts; Control your senses, open your mind. In all it's simplicity. Knock the door, and it will open. But you might struggle to enter the narrow strait gate.

On the broad road, it made crowded. Just follow the flow of people. But on the narrow path, you have to keep your eyes open in rough terrain. There it is slippery, and you can stumble—a place you have to fight and labor fervently. I did. Then the door opened, released. It said so many times, never give up. Do you follow your feelings about how you feel? Then you have lost.

Even parts of psychiatry recognize that pondering can lead to depression. Do you cope with situations? A common expression; are you mentally healthy? One thing is for sure; pain cannot make measured. It made given to each one. Pain is; "that you may be able to bear it, such as it is common to man."

Most people I have met who do not believe in Almighty God. Beyond everything, it relates consistently to their senses. They have a virtual perception of what the world is. In the gaming world, you can put on a virtual helmet, to live in a fixed world, fiction. The senses and emotions do the same, and we live in a cave. We were looking at a wall with shadow movements. To search for truth, look for a cause; light provides shade; follow the light; to the exit of the cave. Out of the cave, the bright made separated from the darkness, and you are in a completely different dimension. This world is real enough. But you must also have enough revelation to see fiction in it all. Reality is real. The animation is the evidence created by man, to a fantasy world, and built on senses and emotions, and a thought.

Pixels are micro, small pieces put together into an image. From the invisible, it can turn into an animated human. Man is of micro-small cells into a whole human being, created in the image of God. After God's likeness. See the simple in the complicated and not complicate in the simple. As Solomon said, "Whoever increases knowledge increases sorrow." Depression is not far away. In the biblical sense, the word knowledge can also mean; acknowledgment. Acknowledgment of the Tree of Knowledge for good and evil became the final step for pure perception. When they eat the fruit, "and they knew they were naked." Knew; to know; knowledge. A computer has a certain number of Giga bites or mega bites.

Once the information of the machine, hardware has reached its saturation point. The device becomes slow and susceptible to viruses. So it is with a human brain as well. Knowledge downloaded can be useful if we have a humble relationship with it.

«Blessed are the poor in Spirit;…»
It is a person who is dependent on an Almighty God as a Creator and Savior. Who doesn't take anyone in captivity? Those who no longer rely on their senses and emotions. Nor on their knowledge. The man did not have access to the fruits of the tree of knowledge from the Almighty Father. The man took it. With the knowledge they saw through their senses, they were naked. With the fear of being seen, feelings, they hid, from that day, the man was in booths, or a net. Our understanding of everything captured him. It can quickly become depressing; We, not made for a complicated life, or in an intricate knowledge.
Man's doctrine of evolution is a dead-end for our development. Therefore, not everyone can follow it. A dead-end means you have to turn around, and go back to the starting point. Until the day you realized you were naked. For me, everything is simple. Don't take everything for granted, and try not to follow everyone else. There are many facts and answers. But one truth beyond everything. The brain; do not have a complete understanding of what is right. Only one mind to download

what it wants. Scientists use the brain for knowledge understanding. One of those who developed the atomic bomb gained knowledge of developing a nuclear weapon. But when he saw the consequences of it he ended up taking his own life. It was more than he could handle. Leave the knowledge to God Almighty because he has given us something more powerful than knowledge.

Wisdom.

Wisdom leads to the right path.
«My son, if thou wilt receives my words, and hide my commandments with thee; So that thou incline thine ear unto wisdom, and apply thine heart to understanding.»
Wisdom; chakam; here has the meaning of reputation, insight, wisdom, and life wisdom, which gives the ability to act way in life's changing situations appropriately. A commandment, whether human or divine. An insight not from intellect but divine.
Understanding; a primitive root; to separate mentally (or distinguish).
So don't include your brain, because wisdom has something to do with revelation and ability to discern.

When wisdom enters your heart, and knowledge is pleasant to your soul.

When I meet Jesus Christ spiritually, no one has to tell me what was wrong or right. It just came to me. It is what wisdom does, and when I read the Bible, it was revealed. Knowledge is something else; it is a learning process. Knowledge from God Almighty comes through wisdom, and it is pleasant.

«Yea, if thou criest after knowledge, and liftest up thy voice for understanding; If thou seekest her as silver, and searchest for her for hid treasures; Then shalt thou understand the fear of the Lord, and find the knowledge of God.»
Seekest her as silver, means also; to strive after:- ask, beg, beseech. So remember, strive to enter at the strait narrow gate. Because if you do not strive to enter it, you shall not be able to reach it.

To see oneself. For the first time. When you struggle to find an answer and end up in Proverbs, a book in the Bible, to discover that the word of God, slap you in your face, figuratively, and see yourself as a fool.
"The fear of the Lord is the beginning of knowledge, but fools despise wisdom and instruction."
A fool; from an unused root; figuratively; silly, foolish. A sadness came over you. When you are a cause of depression and depression is not the cause of you.
Your conscience has taken you back, and open your eyes. To see an Almighty God through Solomon, write a per-

sonal book, "Just for You", and a real pain comes for the day. It is my testimony, not yours. Focus on the redemption of wisdom, not just the fool. Proverbs and Jesus Christ's Parables connected to our conscience. Not an intellectual understanding. The Proverbs fool and the religious Pharisees in Jesus' time go about the same. They blend beliefs, emotions, and mental knowledge into a mess. Without a conscience. Therefore, they cannot walk the narrow path, or strait narrow gate. But wander along the broad road where their perceptions governed. My depression and anxiety opened my eyes to the light or out of the cave if you like.

Jesus Christ says: «For every one that doeth evil hateth the light, neither cometh to the light, lest his deeds should be reproved.»

Inside the light, we find conviction, one who convinces, tells us our fault and even rebukes us. So that our deeds may be made manifest, and that we made wrought in God.

Let's start from the beginning when he regretted the moment he jumped. A miracle, not only that he survived but was allowed to live so that he could witness the remorse. The regret of something he has done. It seems like conscience grabs him when it's too late—but miraculously surviving to show people that jumping is not the right to do it. Some people never go further than depression and anxiety. What about them?

What about me? I was going to leave my testimony alone. But still, you got parts of it. There are contradictions in everything we say and do. Never forget it. It can lead us to something we do not want. We are more proud than we are willing to admit. But I am one of those who believe everything can be for reconstruction and restoration, and when I say faith, I mean fully convinced. Life is not a red carpet; for rich and famous. But to joy and sorrow. The Bible says, "Woe to you that laugh now! For you shall mourn and weep".

My revelation applies to everyone. Remember: There is always someone who has it worse than you, a remarkable conclusion from a man. He jumped into life, after it was too late. By action from thought, and this is a testimony of one who survived.

Ps:
It's never too late.
To live,
and your life will continue
in freedom.

Part Three

Addiction.

How to become drug-related?
It is simple.
Just do it!

The total freedom you get, for the one who is attracted to drug abuse, or alcohol. Freedom to become a slave and a minion. Freedom to be addicted. Freedom to become an empiricist; empiricism; the theory that all knowledge made derived from sense-experience. So, welcome to the world of drug and alcohol addiction. The worst thing you can do to a drug empiricist, is to warn him. Then he will guarantee to do so.
My mom warned my sister and me from the scorching oven when we were young. My sister listens, burned my finger, hard—an empiricist that tested everything without holding on the right things. In Norway, where we live, winter can be hard. Minus twenty degrees. To put your tongue unto ice-cold steel, outside, it is stupidity.

I did after being warned. I guess you find rebelliousness in the empiricist.

But the first time I tried drugs and the freedom I felt, I have never before experienced. The total feeling of being free was very present, and having become addicted, it was that kind of mood I was after. But never found. It is not gold and silver human being are after, but the total feeling of freedom, and that is costly.

Richness.

To have more than you need, and not like Nature, which is pleased with little. Not like a shopping mall pleasing your mind, open up for everything or everybody. Satisfaction is married to addiction. Nature is replacing itself when it's ready for it. Shopping does the same, but end as garbage, and Nature fertilizing itself. More than you need is an addiction, which is very pleasant. Why do I talk about richness and shopping, and not continuing with drugs and alcohol habit? Addiction has an extremely wide specter without satisfaction, no dependency.

Economic crisis

A crack in Norway 1987.

A massive bank collapse. A collapse is better than death. The old cycle was seven good, and seven bad years. Today, economists are embellishing the economy. Adjustment of interest rates. A delicate balance between buying and selling. Fake make-up I would call it. The rest I leave to an economist. The thing is that it is better with a collapse than with a capital six feet under it. Why? Because the flesh is weak, and can't see the consequences. Because of the desire for satisfaction, and without collapse, it will cause death.

In the eighties, after pumping up oil from the North Sea and income flowed into the Bank's bank accounts. It was a boom in that decade, which Norway has never seen. It turned out to be something Norwegians called; yuppie era. Here I come into the picture. Old enough to be a part of it all, but too young to understand the consequence. Old enough to see the possibilities. Opportunities to borrow money for anything you want to do. With high-interest rates and with the promise of high deductions from the authorities. That was the time when we started installing windows with panoramic views. See and be seen.

Everything was glamorous, and no one saw the net behind bushes and scrub. There were warnings, but no one heard, and no one doesn't necessarily mean everyone. There are always some birds that see consequences, and always someone too young to join in the fun. You don't have to be an economist to recognize dangers. For me, the race was almost over before I could start. Yuppie era with girls, wine, and songs. A Norwegian expression for a dissipated life, with a high standard. Eighties hippie era, with my own company, expectations were high, and the opportunities in front of my feet. Blinded by the light is an expression - but true. It all comes for a day, one day. It did it for me, too, is a major collapse. Nothing left, with debt up to my ears, and lots of hard work ahead of me.

To borrow money up to the roof, before it falls, is pretty foolproof. If you want life in the capital, sweep it under the rug. My collapse came to life. A collapse should be part of the economic mindset—a failure to purification and empiric experience. Build a new foundation stone when the old one is outdated. In the construction language in Norway, we say that a building must be rehabilitated every thirty years. Rehabilitation is painful but necessary. Painful because everything must make torn to the bone, only the concrete left. Renewal after a collapse. It is, of course, seen with the eyes of the world. Not with everlasting eyes to an Almighty God. But to open eyes so that one can see the possibilities of collapse and not a final death. Painful there and then, but very redeeming in retrospect. Everything made created well once, not after Fall of Man, where collapse is part of rehabilitation. To teach a child to walk, it must fall sometimes. It's healthy, as long as it's not to death. So the world's future economists will see the importance of collapse, between everything, and the empiricist can learn from the brutal failure.

How long will plastic dominate our lives, before the collapse? The sooner, the better. A collapse is better than

death. Jesus said of his death to his disciples: "The seed must die before it can sprout and give new life."
Nature is satisfied with little, while the world is in a state of satisfaction, to collapse.

How about a beautiful woman in front of a mirror, everyone has seen it, a narcissistic mirror image of themselves. Every time they get a chance to mirror themselves—satisfaction before the collapse. To die from oneself must then be a concept. Something we will come back to it. If you want something and you get it. What is it then? Satisfaction!

Fantasy, what is it? Dreams, fables you can dream away from it, or to. From reality, you are not satisfied with it, or from it. I am a daydreamer, if I drop it, I can travel far. Higher, deeper until there is no one next to it. This kind of daydreaming has an addiction to it. The Bible says, "Bringing into captivity every thought to the obedience of Christ Jesus." Buildings of thought that rise up against an Almighty God. Casting down every imagination, thoughts, and every high thing that exalts itself against the knowledge and acknowledgment against God. Thought buildings, i.e., something you build. Stone for stone, or concrete for concrete. Floor by floor.
Did you know that radio signals are not capable of penetrating concrete? Those with a cell phone know.

What is the film industry today? Is it to give us a message? Or make some money out of it all? Or something much more profound, to deceive the Humane race. Protected with concrete hinder the Truth, to come true. A building of imagination and thoughts. Hollywood, actor under an assumed character. An actor who can deceive, very well. All the impressions we get or have. All the advertising elements in our lives, like Paragliding with background music. Until we think it's possible. Then we jump into life, and the impressions are different than what we first expected. Maybe to disappointment, defeat, and the only thing we have left is: "Nothing is impossible for God Almighty." But we have at least tried. Impressions of disappointment can quickly become a trademark, for some, but everything is possible for God.

Sexuality.

Almighty God creates Man and Woman after His image, a representative figure, in His likeness. He created us with a desire so strong that we can multiply ourselves, to fill the earth. To become one, to Glory and Holiness. Not to our satisfaction. Sexuality after the Fall: Fall of Man has become an addiction and not Glory and Holiness. Hence overcrowding. The human race has come out of the framework of God Almighty. We live in a desire for satisfaction, not a balanced desire to multiply. We are filling the earth, to be just enough. Holiness and Glory are in a stable order. Sexual addiction is to disorder and confusion. Overcrowding. An imbalance to collapse, or worse, dead.

Culture collapse.

The Western world has a perception that it is the impoverished continent that is the cause of overpopulation governed and controlled by their culture, and the poverty of the Third World. It won't end until you make fewer children—a very narrow view of a world problem.

Researchers in biology have found that when a sperm enters an egg cell, then through advanced microscopes, a powerful glow of light can be seen, with the sperm and egg cell becoming one. When God Almighty said: Let there be light; it became light, and when life comes into being, you see a glimmer of light come to life. Of course, the researchers explain this flash of light with a chemical reaction, thus denying the life that made created in the flash of light. They are not able to see the right color. When addiction comes, they get blind. Blind is to be in darkness. In the sun, you can see colors; without light, it is impossible to see anything. So when a glimmer of light comes to life, with arguments like: we are too many. We only see the chemical reaction.

On the other hand, where culture is more important than common understanding, children are their future retirement. Not a child born into a glimmer of light. A world where intellectual understanding is worth a lifeless than knowledge of life itself, or in a world where a child is just a tool for his or her pension. So culture shock is when cultures crash into each other to a flash of light into a collapse. A glow of fire flares up into the darkness, in its little understanding. Then the net is set up for failure.

Imbalance is when someone has lost balance. It is instead an instability that prevents us from seeing what is right. All humankind depends on understanding how everything has made together, either primitive or advanced, understanding, but it goes for the same. Everything we made caught up in our knowledge is only God's revealed hands that can set us free.

Science is pornographic bed literature. Why? Because it is satisfying for one's intellect. In the brain there is software. Where you can download what you want, and create an understanding of conviction. Because you want it, knowledge can be an excellent ballast. It must never rule but have a humble relationship with it. If you let it rule, you will one day be able to believe, for nothing. Therefore, Jesus Christ says:" Those who see shall be blind." In the obvious sense, blindness is darkness.

Someone needs to say, "Be light." So that people can see. It is evident in the day. Life needs light. That's why I leave science behind. Not informative knowledge, but all theoretical claims. Big Bang Theory. Everything made created in order. One after the other. Depending on the One, and God Almighty is excellent. More significant than my intellect. Never be discouraged, but believe, and you will see it. Nothing is more significant than a sunrise. When it lights up, and you can see everything.

Addiction is more than a word. Addiction is tacky, stuck, not to get loose, and to top it all off, you want it. To say everything is a balance, the Golden Balance is a lie; it is about free will to make a choice. It doesn't stop there but the decision to choose, to go. Make a decision.

There are people I have met; they where heavily addicted to alcohol, in and out of hospitals and institutions. Anonymous alcoholics, and I don't know what. The person has everything an alcoholic can experience. Desperate parents. Broken relationship. Financial ruin. They lost their driver's license, just to mention something. When you know alcoholism; First, it takes time and realizes that you are addicted. Then they go a long way before they do anything about it, from what I know best, to humble surrender. A person I knew made a choice, raised his hands to an Almighty God, took a grip in his life, and got a strong presence with Jesus Christ. New life. New opportunities. With the testimony of what an Almighty God did in his life. Set free. Short specific words. With power in it. Nothing is more uplifting than that. Experiencing a ride can quickly become a downturn. It is for a reason Jesus says, "We must build on a rock." Getting intense experiences at a distance can be a threat in itself. He started advertising the exemption from alcohol. The liberation was so convincing that he took the liberty of drinking light beer. Light beer, in Norway is a beer type with meager alcohol percentage. As a substitute. It went on for a period and proclaimed to other alcoholics, on the foundation of being set free. But the foundation was built on sand; sand has no solid ground in it, and with a lot of adversity. He was torn down, as to say. A new round of hospitals and institutions. It is allowed to fall. With the fall, it is possible to rise again.

But what does he do when he has risen again. Other than blaming the circumstances and everyone else. A tragic outcome from one who fell sharply, and against an Almighty God, powerful enough to set people free. In Greek philosophy, it becomes the word moderation; it usually denotes an ability or will to control their desires and lust. The Greek word for desire is; epithymnia; can be translated into; Prudence: For me, a desire for something. There is a difference between one's own will and free will. Therefore, a Golden Balance is a lie. A balance between light and dark. Hot and cold.

This type of philosophical balance is a big lie. Either or is basic. God's way does not go in a yoke with anyone or anything.

Acknowledgment.

Several books about addiction have been written. Up and down in mind. Accessible, thorough, big heavy books. Everything for every taste. But there is one thing all this falls back to it, and that is the acknowledge of being dependent. Some call the addiction allergy; you just can't stand it. Do you have severe peanut allergy; you die, worst case. It is where the acknowledgment of addiction must be. Without acknowledging, it will not be progressive. The alcoholic does not need a developmental doctrine of alcohol, but a revelation in a confession, the easiest way in simplicity. It is heavy enough in itself. A burden is to carry something substantial because it weights it.

In Norway, there were strict laws against the use and sale of marijuana and hashish. In fact, throughout Scandinavia, but there was a small Freetown, by ferry to Copenhagen. The capital of Denmark. All marijuana and cannabis smokers could go there. A Freetown. A small community or maybe call it a village. In the capital. A haven for unfolding. There you could buy cannabis freely in different varieties—user equipment; hash pipe.

Find a local pub, and freely smoke hashish and drink cold Danish beer—this feeling of freedom not found in Scandinavia. Get there, have a blast, and become "stone," to unfold in a small community. Where everything looked "very well." A society with accepted satisfaction for addiction. There the community was free. So far. Legalization goes no further than that; God created not plants for abuse, and one day was enough, enough. A society without rules disappeared. Norwegians back where they came from it. Where is the freedom of addiction? One does not become physically addicted to cannabis, they say. But the pursuit of stimuli, it is not possible to be free. Everything has its price, and there are no winners in legalization—just a big net, with apathy, a diagnosis of long-term use. Acknowledgment, confess. Freetown Christiania is Copenhagen's alternative neighborhood today.

Acknowledge your weakness. You are strong when you know your weakness. A weakness of what? Weakness not to bother your laziness? Weakness is an abused word. The opposite of weak is strong. Secure in what way? The confusion seems not far away when you ask yourself questions. Confusion is the same as a disorder; in the biblical term. Put things in order. Acknowledgment; accept or admit. First step. Next step; the other foot following; start walking. Here comes the confusion, when you are stuck into a net. Not able to move, and do not move, you will be more into it.

Accept your weakness. Weak in itself. Acknowledge; confess. "Confess your faults one to another…". Your confession makes you durable. It has to made revealed from a revelation. Otherwise, your acknowledge is not there. Humbleness is surely part of this book. Suppose you are abroad and lost in a city. Do you try to get out of there by yourself? With a map, or ask someone? Ask. "The effectual fervent prayer of a righteous man avails much." Prayer is also; request; ask for…Righteousness is a statue, visible for anyone. Righteousness should be a cornerstone of us like Jesus Christ is for us. He poured out His blood for us. Blood is life for the unrighteous one. Acknowledgment is to admit. A primitive root, from the tree of knowledge, of good and evil, acknowledges; can also be; be sure, of a surety. The acknowledgment in Eden's garden was there no need for that word because the Fall of Man was not attending yet, and the tree of knowledge is still standing by itself. Philosophers acknowledge, also called freedom condition. Usually end up in a Freetown, for those who can't stop to an end station for addiction.
A net you never will get out of unless you confess your acknowledgment.

Poverty.

We can become poor or be pleased with little. Poverty soaked into this world system. It is part of a net. Do you desires what others have? Or are you satisfied with what made given? What taken is taken. What's given is given. Poverty can be an exquisite word for the rich. The question is; whether the rich can write about poverty. Every economist or politician knows deep down in his heart: there must be some poverty in society, for society to be sustainable. The exploitation opportunities will always be there. Denial of this statement will be steadfast in any form of media, for a politician. No one dares to say: Be pleased with little.
Some have made themselves weak by wanting more than they can have the opportunity to have. The word of God dares to say what a politician refuses to answer. «But godliness with contentment is great gain. For we brought nothing into this world, and we can certainly carry nothing out».

Everything is relative, someone said. In a world full of acidification and pollution. Made climate change or not. Remember: To be pleased with little is not poverty; it is something you choose. You do not choose poverty. It is a condition you just have to live. Self-indulgent or not. A situation you become addicted to without being able to get away from it. An addict may stop intoxicated. That can't a poor one do. Addiction is poverty in itself. An addict in itself can stop being intoxicated. Jesus Christ said, «For ye have the poor always with you;…»

I have seen poor, rich in Jesus Christ: The way, life, and the truth. It can change any perception of how one is feeling.

In Norway, the majority are wealthy, with debt up to the limit. And they are committed to spending time to pay it, poverty in itself. They can sell everything. Released from debt, but the money just spent on something else.

Then it comes; To be pleased with little is a big win. Are you planning the future, or are you living? Day by day. But one thing I wonder, what can you get out of poverty? Buying or selling is not on the list of poorness.

«Pure religion and undefiled before God and Father in Heaven is this, to visit fatherless and widows in their affliction, and to keep himself unspotted from the world.» Say it like this; Affliction is an anguish burdened persecution of tribulation of every kind of trouble.

If you are miserable, you are trapped. As well you are into it or out of it. In poverty doesn't matter where you are. But one thing for sure, you are addicted to it, and it is no one more into alcohol and drugs, than those trapped into poverty. Strange enough because where do they get the money for it. To make it simple, in poverty, it is the family's who struggle with the misery. Father drink and their mother suffer, and it is widespread. We know this; The rich one says.

Pure and undefiled before God is to visit fatherless and widows in their affliction, I will say.

Welcome to The Shopping Center after this. Where greediness is not pleased with anything, and not like Nature, which is pleased with little. Poverty is a wake-up call for the rich, not the poor.

As they say, "First the rich strive to become rich, and then strive not to lose it again."

You can't find more poverty than that. Poverty means; The state of being extremely poor, the misery of neediness, and hardship against being poor.

 Because you say: says Jesus Christ; I am rich, have become wealthy, and need nothing; and do not know that you are wretched, miserable, poor, blind and naked, Jesus Christ continue, He counsel you to buy from Him since you are rich and have money to buy; gold refined in the fire, that you may be rich; and white garments, that you may be clothed, that the shame of your nakedness may not reveal; and anoint your eyes with eye-salve that you may see.

The poverty in your richness will make the poor in you rich. So the result of poverty in richness is addiction. Welcome to the cruel world, as to say—poverty as an announcement.

We are not broke.

We spend time with people, entertainment for the lost, and it's not funny. I have met poor unjust people, and the poor one who turns the other cheek. You find justice in every camp, and with love, you can be standing—the right to the end.

Jesus Christ said in one of his eschatological speeches: "And because iniquity shall abound, the love of many shall wax cold." Do not believe poverty should escape. When Jesus Christ speaks of the tribulation of the end time, it is not about poverty alone. But part of an image, an addiction that soaked into a big picture.
«For then shall be great tribulation, such as was not since the beginning of the world to this time, no, nor ever shall be.»
Imagine tribulation on top of poverty. It will be more than they can bear. That's why these days should make shortened; Therefore, you will find in all history books where there has been tribulation. It's a cruel world, and it's the world to blame.
The Greek word for tribulation; of the verb thlibo; which originally means; crush, press; secondly; make straight, narrow. In the transferred sense, it is used about life's difficulties and hardships. Tribulation belongs to the conditions of life for men; it is a judgment of God placed on a sinful humankind. It is a natural consequence of sin, and everyone, both evil and good, has more or less part.

What does poverty do to us that we are not affected by it? Only indirectly. Such as slavery in America. Jesus

Christ does not depart from the truth, or socialism in Northern Europe, fighting for their rights. When they get what they fight for, they open up to cheap labor from Eastern Europe. The picture is complex. Not necessarily poverty. But love has grown cold, among most, giving some less so they can get more themselves.

Status quo the existing state of affairs, especially government social or political issues. To maintain the status quo is to keep things the way they presently are.

Alcoholism.

Alcoholism is to maintain the status quo; to keep the thing the way they presently are.

At the time of writing this book, I get a message that a friend of mine is dead. Alcohol kills. This is a war. The brutal truth must instead be hammered on the table. Most people who drink lose their home and family. While the alcoholic is addicted to alcohol, the alcoholic makes his closest dependence on them. Self-pity is a weapon, developing sympathy for the relatives how they become available when the alcoholic needs them. When an epidemic breaks out, the first thing they need to find is the symptoms; and diagnosis, the same symptoms the same disease without exception. All drug addicts will rebuke you as soon as you tell them about their addiction. They convince you because they have full control. With intoxicants, you also find persuasive manipulative convincing.

They convince the belief that everything is "very well."
Therefore, they are good at getting into conflict: even
self-righteousness, pride, and arrogance. An alcoholic is
now related to; alcohol use disorder, and disorder is confusion.

An addict once said to me: "I like to live on the edge because then I don't occupy too much space." An irony that
you don't see the seriousness of it.

Those who fall from "the edge," one foot out, and another after. Will land so hard that they usually don't survive.
It is a sad truth. Some are more related to intoxication
than others, according to scientists. But don't forget a
thing, we have free will to choose. Where do the
thoughts come from it? The Bible tells of the one who
built his house on sand, and the house fell, and great was
the fall of it—all for the sake of convenience. Science
often looks for etheric physical, a rational explanation
for the most part, and often they fall short. A shovel is no
longer a shovel.

"God stands against the proud, but give grace to the
humble."

Because pride stands against God, and everyone, a conflict maker, who is everyone to blame?

The world wants explanations for the most part, but the
simple is often the best. Humility means; to bend. Make
himself less than himself. There is no resistance there—
no "Against."

"Confess your faults one to another, and pray one for another, that ye may be healed. The effectual fervent prayer of a righteous man availeth much».

To confess is interesting because it also means; to acknowledge or agree fully; confess, profess, give thanks, promise. When you are effective, decide to be active and efficient in deciding to get out of it—a powerful commitment, and God sees to heart. Just have a fervent heart.

In my youth, I start smoking cigarettes, and it became a habit. I didn't hide it either. Until my grandmother's sadness came over me and told me a story about a man in her job as a pharmacist: "He tries to stop smoking, and nothing happens. One day, he said, from Today, I am the Boss over you and not you the Boss over me. Since then, he stopped smoking».

Why is our physical body so strong. It's like a shopping mall open to everyone and everything, and let the body consider what it's like it. Not you. But Today I am the Boss.

Over the cigarettes.

Over the alcohol,

and over the drugs

What next…?

It's always something, addiction rules. In this world, nothing left. As I said earlier for satisfaction, we will make this planet dead and a desert. You have sucked out the life of living water, nothing left, only imbalances, and self pithiness. You say you don't recognize this in your life. That's because arrogance usually doesn't. Before a collapse. Not to death.

What do you vote for an election? For your own best? Or for your neighbor and your country?

Alcohol kills in one way or another in the name of satisfaction addiction.

In this planet we live in, has a saturation point. Pollution is nothing but that of many pollutants with the same product at the same time. In a chemical imbalance that Nature is unable to break down. The same with the body. Too much carbohydrate makes you overweight for most people. Biochemical is when it is no longer degradable. The Word of God says: "... and should destroy them which destroy the earth". To put it this way: When it is not degradable, it is no longer a collapse but a death. Destroy; also; to rot thoroughly; to ruin; corrupt; perish. Earth is a substantial part or the whole of the terrain globe. Including the occupants in each application. Clear understanding, meaning us.

This is not a scare propaganda but a fact. To destroy is not to collapse but death.

In my work as a painter, where oil paints used, solvent damage was quite common. The body is capable of breaking down the toxins. You just needed fresh air over time. But over time, the saturation point is reached. The cup is full. The chronic solvent damage became a diagnosis they had to live with it. So it is a saturation point in everything; ended, something can be sudden and brutal. To finish while «the game is good,» not one foot out and the other after it.

To finish; quite; accomplish. Finish to an end. Finish, to be completed. The never-ending story is to take a stand, finish it once and for all, and say: "Today I am the Boss. Over ..."

To accomplish it, once and for all.

Drugs.

Drugs are illegal. So why do they do it? Because the image of reality is similar to an adventure, and it's not scary for those who dare. When something is forbidden, rules are there to break. It's not just the rebelliousness in you, but the adventurer too. On walking in a landscape, you think no one has been before you. Some flee from something. Some escape to something, others both. Who are these people? They are different. Like the drugs they choose. Each one's taste. Now we talk in time, before addiction. Before, the offenses have become a habit, the explorer in unexplored terrain. It is not primarily about drugs, but to achieve a climax of satisfaction. Mount Everest is not far away. I have been there. Done that; has been said so many times to the pathetic. The intoxication is related to so many. From growing up into drunkenness and crime. To the narcissist who wants to intoxicate into a grandiose self-image.

No one is the same. It's not the drugs either—a candy store. Every taste seems different. Depending on who it is. In chemistry, the chemicals react differently to one another. Some are exploding. Others spread out smells. We know that the individual can be complicated, but let's stay in the realm where the emotions are still good. The melancholy has not come over us yet. The paranoia has not, however, taken hold. Yet. All side effects do not yet come true. Let's still stay in Paradise, before we discovered we were naked. In Paradise, when we did not hold anything. Before, we had to hide from the Almighty God and understand having done something wrong before we ate of the fruit of the tree of knowledge, good and evil. Right before we realized it was pleasant to the eyes. The fruit to be desired to make one wise. For a moment. In this atmosphere, some of us will live. Before we discover that we are naked, and in the name of the Law become criminals. Disobedient, and at the moment, we leave "Legalize It." For the moment, because the consequences come later, and we also ridicule, "anything that can happen will happen." Here in this Paradise, everyone has been. Especially drug addicts. So please don't blame them because it was pleasant to the eyes. It was a delightful, delectable, goodly pleasant precious thing.

Sometimes things take you, and suddenly you're not in Paradise anymore, because of the precious things. God works with people; people work with things, and make them addicted, to be free and free will. It is like night and day. Don't let "The Twilight Zone" take you.

A Poet gives you pictures, not words. They just use words to express their images. He created in His images, His likeness. God almighty is; a performer, especially; a poet, doer.
When He said, «thou shalt not…». Do not do is meant by action, and by action, you are a doer.
«But be ye doers of the word, and not hearers only, deceiving your self.»
Do not do, be a doer, not to do. But doer not to…?!
«For if any be a hearer of the word and not a doer, he is like an unto a man beholding his natural face in a glass (mirror): For he beholdeth himself, and goeth his way, and straightway forgetteth what manner of man he was.»
Become a Poet who made given a Picture, an Image in His likeness. Instead, we do what we should not do, and here the empiricists go again. We want back to Paradise, which is not there anymore.

The big deception after being satisfied more. In the meantime, Nature is satisfied with little. They were waiting for something to happen. Hopefully, to collapse and not to death. Drug dealers and users. Side by side. One is no worse than the other. Because at the bottom rank, they switch to being both. But the community is addicted.

They are interrelated, but you rarely find friendship because the addiction is so strong. But when the addicted is no longer there. After another detox, and out of the environment. Then the feeling of friendship returns. The addiction is cunning. Like the Devil. Accusations and divisions. From the freedom to be free from intoxication.

«For the good I that would I do not: but the evil which I would not, that I do. Now, if I do that, I would not, it is no more I that do it, but sin dwelleth in me».

Some say, "My flesh is weak, so why to care." And obey the frailty in itself.

Jesus Christ say: "Strive to enter the strait gate."

Strive to struggle to enter the narrow gate, and the expression "Never give up" blows away like the wind.

Jesus Christ also say, "Lean on me," but without your will, you cannot lean on anything at all.

Other than going back where you are not going. Remember, Paradise is no longer there.

Just some "friends." They have something they can sell you so that everything can be as before.

On a Charter trip or a Cruise ship. All as it pleases. Man is still on the move, in mind, or the surroundings. It never end. In and out of prisons. In the name of the Law, since it is not yet "Legalized."

But one day in the name of the profit.

My great-grandfather gambled away his farm and land,
what was left, he drank up in homemade liquor.
But if he hadn't, someone else would have done the
same. We look at the circumstances. Not on the facts.
An era is over, and you will always find Freetown.
Somewhere out there.

Independent Day.

4 July 1776. The Declaration of Independence.

When Christopher Columbus discovered America and
the Bahamas, he met an Independent people who shared
what they had. Columbus later wrote about this in his
logbook: "They gave us parrots and balls of cotton and
spears and many other things ... They willingly traded
barter with all their possessions. They did not carry
weapons nor know them. I showed them a sword; they
grabbed it in the egg and cut it because of ignorance.
They had no iron. Their spears are of sugar cane; they
would become excellent servants. With fifty men, we
could conquer them all and get them to do everything we
want".

Free people. They were not after gold and silver, how
Columbus and his people were. They were satisfied with
little, and what they had they shared. If there were con-
flicts with other tribes, they fought, of dissatisfaction and

not on orders from captains or kings. In all its simplicity. It was not a paradise. They were people discontinued from it. But with its Independence. To Columbus and the Spaniards came. The greed that is never satisfied with anything, and eventually malls open to everything and everyone—having conquered a people, a country with its Independent life. Thus began 500 years ago the story of the European invasion of the Native American settlements in America after conquest, slavery, and death. The story of Columbus Today lives under mediating circumstances as a Hero. When it comes to the point of view, we know the truth as long as we are willing to acknowledge it.

Let's not make our Independence hero worship. It is how the knowledge made the Spaniards superior. But knowledge makes addiction, as conquest is for the benefit all the people involved expect to receive, and the most fabulous thing is, "Say it, so no one understands it."
You can lie about the past. Close up to the truth. Or you can omit relevant facts that can lead to unacceptable conclusions before relevant facts.
Words are noble but can write down on a gray stone, without life but hard enough to hit someone in the head. Or on a wooden board that deteriorates and eventually burns. It's not life made. But precious word on the precious metal. For deep understanding and eternity in it, and it live every time you touch the word. God's Word of

Wisdom. Proverbs. From the Poet himself; "... let there be light ...".

The addiction to having an understanding. Knowledge. All this used to conquer something or someone. It is Independent Day in almost every country in the world. To lift the Independence of a glorification is idolatry, and nationalism.
The Tower of Babel means confusion. "So the Lord scattered them abroad from there over the face of all the earth."
To Independence, the world has not seen the like and duly celebrated. From colonization to a dominant superpower.
In conclusion, the world made explained from the standpoint one stands.

"War is healthy for the state," a radical writer once said. What is a war for it? War for peace? A declaration of Independence. What is sin? Stealing from others? Stealing the Other Took: Eve took, and ate the fruit from the Tree of Knowledge. Then she saw that she was naked. War is ultimately about creating, giving peace. So who are the victors, other than those with the Declaration of Independence? An a Independent Day they can celebrate.

My independent realized life turned into an emptiness, and a question. What do we do in the middle of all this?

In the world we took. Who is entitled to what? Big questions in a small book about Fowler's Net. My conclusion and revelation are that we have become dependent on our Independence. We claim everything. So why not be pleased with little.
The greatest freedom I have experienced is my total addiction to an Almighty God - Jesus Christ.
After being released from a dependent world. Which still tells me about my addiction.
I am in the potter's hands, in His Likeness and Image.
This can no one take away from me.

In a welfare state, one always finds a Freetown. It made customized to each one for addiction, and when Independence has come to power, for control, in Fowler's net.
"They speak a language challenging enough to imprison the brave in the flock. But neither provocative that it incites them to fights they cannot win or so threatening that it will arouse the wrath of the ruling powers."
In Independence of Freedom, addiction is always there.
Under the Independence of freedom, we find slavery, oppression, and death.
We are nothing but: "Another brick in the wall."
The understanding of freedom Today is a wolf in sheep's clothing, and the only thing we can fight is ourselves.
What did we learn during addiction? Independent Day comes first under obedience to an Almighty God. To Jesus Christ.

Freedom is when we have the wisdom to understand that we made created in God's image and His parable.
In Him - Jesus Christ, who will set you free; Indeed.

Part Four

Freedom.

"If the Son, Jesus Christ, therefore shall make you free, ye shall be free indeed." Free is not a slave and indeed is, really; certainly, clean, surely, verily, of a truth. Finally, and certainly; Indeed.

You probably have driven your car in the street in a city, where it's says on a gate you passing: Don't block the driveway. Hindrance, whatever it is, which prevents you from passing. Freedom is not to block other people's doors, instead to make the gate clear.

To make a path in the forest is hard work. Work with your salvation is the same. What about Grace? Grace made given, already, because you will not perish before judgment day. Almighty God has already given us free will; to chose which path we will walk into. It is Grace over Grace. Jesus Christ gave His life for all sinners. So all humanity can be able to receive through our choices.

Free will is freedom, freedom to chose eternal life with Father in heaven and Jesus Christ His only begotten Son, or eternal life without God Almighty, where they are crying and gnashing of teeth. This is not freedom when you are rebellious, the humble one, He will give mercy.

Free will is based on humankind choices between good and evil.

"Thou shalt break them with a rod of iron; thou shalt dash them in pieces like a potter's vessel." Dash them in pieces; cause to be discharged—Potter's vessel; Creator versus creation. The Creator has made everything. He is not an evolution. He is able to create, to dash the nature in pieces—God create, not rebellion.
When you have been trapped into something, and then released again, you sense freedom. First, when you lose it, you know it. Not only that, but you also worship freedom even more, when you got it back.

When Jesus Christ says: You will be free totally. It is the Almighty God's plan. He will restore everything into what made meant to be. In Part four it about releasing in life, to those who chose to be humble, God give grace. It is about love and taking authority in your life with Jesus Christ at your side.

Let's go back to Grace; Grace is dangerous when it comes in wrong hands: One time saved always saved. Grace is confusion for those who haven't understood the freedom in Christ. They become deceived. The Christianity of Christ doesn't live righteously anymore, because of abused Grace, it is sectarian, and control, not freedom. The worst thing is, they act like Grace is a person. Make a relationship with Jesus, then you will understand. As I already said: Satisfaction is an addiction; that is Grace in a nutshell, and certainly a hindrance to be free indeed.

Socialism

In a pencil drawing of Walter Crane from 1885, capitalism made portrayed as a vampire that exploits the worker. On the wings of the vampire stands Religious hypocrisy and Party politics. Socialism comes as a saving angel with the hat of freedom and the torch of enlightenment. Bible says: "And no marvel; for Satan himself is transformed into an angel of light." Light; to show or make known one's thoughts, or shining angel a torch of enlightenment. All Ism is a delight for those who are attached to it. As an angel of light.

Socialism, the root in the Latin sociare, which means to combine or to share. Societas; This latter word could mean companionship and fellowship and the more legalistic idea of a consensual contract between freemen. Freemen; a person who is not a slave or serf. Before addiction. Freedom in captivity. A Platonic community, governed by the state. Principalities, powers, and rulers of the darkness of this world. An angel of light blinds them and they deceive men. Promises and they lift Human beings, without any Almighty God, which is idolatry, worshiping an idol. It said once: It is not communism who will ruin capitalism, but capitalism itself. The same goes for socialism. The consequence is a fact, into socialism net or even better, snare. Socialism makes people lacy and ungodly.

You will find socialist, which fear for being blind because they lost their freedom to see, but to lose your spiritual freedom to see is worst. If your eyes is dark, you only have your physical eyes left, to view, whatever. There comes a time when all Isms have played their part, and then everything is put right. Ruined from the inside, from itself, which is the most devastating for a nation. They are waiting for a new Ism. The emperor's new clothes, never let wait. That doesn't fables do either. "And they shall turn away their ears from the truth and shall be turned unto fables."

The freedom of the created, from the established. Is now freedom in an intellectual understanding of what is right, and we are finally being caught off. Freedom tastes best; the first time you flavor it, and suddenly, you are dependent on it.

Socialism in Norway, which revolted with capitalism and the church. What kept the people down with their prejudices and doctrines. Today, socialism has opened up to Islam. Ungodliness and religions will always goes hand in hand.

Jesus Christ was crucified by soldiers of the Roman Empire but sentenced to death by the Pharisees, the Israel religious leaders. Jesus was bold towards them and therefore sentenced to death. Hate, even Jesus taught them to love the enemies. This is is what he said to the people about the Pharisees and the scribes:" All therefore whatsoever they bid you observe, that observe and do, but do not ye after their works; for they say, and do not." Israel viewed the Roman Empire as ungodly, while the Roman Empire saw the Israel leaders as religious, and in a revealed picture, these would always go hand in hand. The religious Pharisee is found in the human race at all times. Always present. Independent of everything.

Fear

One of my best-labored colleagues I have had was an African Muslim. One project we had was the exterior facade of a five-floor residential block, where the lift needed outside the facade. To my surprise, this man was terrified at the moment we were on our way up. I asked if he was scared. He did not answer. Then I looked at him and said: What are you afraid of it? Don't you believe in Islam? Yes, he responded. So is it not heaven in

Islam? Yes. So what are you afraid of it? I asked. «Because I don't live by Islamic law, and it doesn't make me worthy of getting there,» he replied, and this he said, clinging to a lift five floors above the ground. Fear, and condemnation, is the fruit of all the religions. Custodial and control. Diabolos; devil; accusations, divisions, slander, and the father of all lies, this he is "good" at it. There is no love in religion.

Jesus Christ said: "Love your enemies. Bless them that curse you and pray for them which despitefully use you, and persecute you". No religions have this, just rules, and no freedom. Like the culture they don't see it, they only live it and Fowler's net is next.
There is no fear in love; but perfect love casts out fear, because fear involves torment. He who fears has not been made perfect in love. Let's put the words in order. Fear; also means terror, exceedingly fear, troublemaker, holy terror. Love, the more profound word of love, is; to be a friend to; Unconditionally, despite everything. Torment means; penal infliction; punishment—the term, perfect; to complete; another word; to be complete with the Lord.
So there is no fear in love. On the other hand, fear causes terror—terrifying people. Terror kills. "And do not murder" is a statement in The New Covenant with Jesus Christ since you shall love your enemy. Because when you have love, you become unconditional friends with it,

and it never fails with no punishment. Finishing and ful-
fill the race of love altogether. Perfectly. The righteously
in Christ will see the Kingdom of God Almighty. Fear is
unbelief. Fear is the oppression of conviction. They are
convinced in their head and not in their heart, and the net
is complete.

Fear is not common sense. Fear captivates you. You are
trapped like anxiety, and learn you to live with it away
from freedom—and away from peace and love. Fear is
flesh and spirit not the Holy Spirit. The flesh is human
nature, carnal. But if you are led by The Holy Spirit, you
are not under the law. The works of the flesh are manifest, fear is human nature, and you find it in any religion-
oppressed idolatry and fear is not a part of the fruit of
The Holy Spirit. Freedom makes free. So the conclusion
is: There is no fear in love.

Fear of God.

"The fear of the Lord is the beginning of knowledge: but
fools despise wisdom and instruction." Instruction; also
meaning; discipline.

Those who smoke, drink, and claw each other wherever.
Blows nicotine into your face and says: You know,
everything is just by Grace. It is what we call Abused
Grace—once saved, always saved. How, then, can we
gain insight into what Jesus said? We talk about the

Grace, just as we do with a person. But Grace is not a person but an expression that we are not condemned for our deeds until Jesus returns; "to judge the living and the dead."
"Endure unto the end, the same shall be made saved," is a fact and not a suggestion.

I've met drug addicts on weaning in an institution where they told me that they have met Christians who have made them a prayer of salvation. A kind of confession that they saved to the faith of Jesus Christ, and that was the end of the story. Not been renewed, just brought the old life into the new and the last one was worse than the first. The freedom they got was more and longer into captivity. They are moving into a network where everything got worse and the word "free indeed" was gone like the dew for the sun. An abused Grace can lead you to "a sentence of death." Lack of Fear of the Lord is no beginning of knowledge. Either acknowledgment. There is no wisdom in foolishness and it is lack of discipline.

Remember we are created in His Image we are the potter's vessel. It should have been enough to be humble.
Be not wise in thine own eyes: fear the Lord, and depart from evil, the Lord says.
There is only one thing to say about lacking the fear of God: Welcome to the self-righteous world.

The Bible cannot read black and white, as it stands. But read black and white with a red thread in it, and the red ribbon must be revealed; revelation is life. It is unity because it comes from the word of God. Same mind because it is from the same.

Faith.

Faith, faithfulness, full confidence, faithfulness one cannot be unfaithful. Faithful is to be faithful throughout the person's being. Relate entirely without deviations. Nonconformity is adultery. Faith is full of confidence. So to rely solely upon and without no doubt on the person's being and what he says. Infidelity is a sin; faith is not an easy confession. But faith is to say yes to the whole person's being. A marriage, to "Death separate them." But also faith in Jesus Christ, a promise of eternal life. So how can you be unfaithful? Faith convinced of something you have seen. A presence with someone who says: Love your enemies unconditional, despite everything.

Righteousness.

Suppose you pull off the feather of a dead bird, and it is only the skin left. Life comes from inside since the blood is poured out. From inside, if your life is alive, you are alive; You were living with feathers and wings. You can fly. There is no short cut in understanding simple mind;

Simple answer. Society's real democracy gives us promises when it comes to freedom. Democracy is that plural one rules. What about the minority? Their opinion can't do anything in the minority. They have to follow the crowd, or fight against, and be oppressed. Freedom to speak that might be.

Speak what the plural democracy likes to hear. Democracy is an illusion, an illusion of what is right. It made based on what humans think is right. Based on people's point of view. Righteousness is something else—respect for the plural agreement you might do, speak freely. But for what reason. What the heart is full of, will come out of your mouth. To see our self is the last thing we do. Plural or minority is the only question of our choice. Without righteousness, democracy will fail, and Bible says: "As it is written, there is none righteous, no, not one." So democracy will fail, sad to say, but truth. A President in the USA said once: "It is not what the country does for you, but what you do for the country." Today seems like the opposite. Corruption kills, we know that. If the country is corrupt, what then? "For righteousness sake." But do the "right" thing can be a trap. It can be religious or cultural, from a doctrine, you learned to act from it. Jesus Christ called the Scribes and the Pharisees for hypocrites. The root of the Greek word, hypocrites, is; an actor under an assumed character. What is your personality?

Some places in Africa, children are kidnapped and trained to be child soldiers. These poor children has no basis for what is right and wrong, after they have been brainwashed by the guerrilla over an period of time. The children are kidnapped only for one reason; to become fearless killers. Some children rescued from the claws of the guerrillas, and you ask them how this is possible? Right up to the kids respond: "The first time, something did resistance in us. We knew it was wrong. That resistance eventually disappeared." With more lives on the conscience they only fought for the "cause." In a resistance movement. With a conscience, who first resisted.

God created us, in his image, in his parable. With a conscience. Under the auspices of sin, it dies, and the conscience dies, the Spirit of God dies. Therefore God said to the first man in the Garden of Eden: "If you eat of the Tree of Knowledge, you will surely die." In the fall of sin, the Tree of Knowledge becomes a substitute for survival, not for living. On the Tree of Knowledge, togetherness died with an Almighty Creator God. Without a living God, it flourished a religious, cultural, and intellectual understanding of what is "right." Therefore, Jesus Christ, the Son of God, says: I will "indeed" set you free. We do not get off the stain unless we get a deep understanding of the word, indeed—a revelation. One revelation is to open a Christmas present and finally see what it contains. Revelation; comes into view. Become visible from the hidden. Physically, we must have blood in us to keep us alive until we die. Eventually, we learned to live for ourselves. But without a living creative Almighty God.

In a democracy, one elected, in a dictatorship, just take it. Out of the same, we become different. But most people I have met behave as if they are alive forever. Down here on this planet. The proverbs say, "there is an eternity in us all", and that's not to be avoided. The cornerstones, to have faith, is to believe. To live forever, then no one can die. Then justice must be a "must"—righteousness built on faith. "Love your God with all your heart, and your neighbor as yourself". In a heart, it pumps blood. A life. A place to live. With a living creative Almighty God, and Jesus Christ, the Son of God. Because our narrow field of view is very local, it is only with wisdom for the deep understanding of righteousness; we come to our "right." Not angled into a knowledge of this world, from the Tree of Knowledge.

All knowledge is from God Almighty.
But it was not given, we took it.

The lack of humility, above all, understanding. Do we become or remain in injustice? In righteousness, there must be humility. They belong together.

Solomon said in his day, "knowledge is pain." To put it that way, he humbly experienced that after seven hundred wives, and idolatry. He left a picture of what could happen. Being deprived of freedom means that we have a zealous God. A potter's Father. Knowledge is pain. Do you want to submit or become submissive? The dilemma of freedom. But never forget this; you have not created yourself, or based on evolution. There will be an injustice to such people. Unrighteousness gives a bitter taste and adapts instead; in "right and wrong"; insight into one's understanding.

Democracy will never come to its "right" because this world lies in evil. Lying means having a narrow view, not being able to move; wicked can turn into anything. Justice is not just a symbol. But wisdom beyond everything. The majority will never come to a revelation, but dispute what is "right": It is not what democracy does for you, but what you do for democracy.

Obsession.

Here are three different stories,
with the same starting points.
Out of the same, but with different outcomes.

A story from birth to terror:

A little boy is born in a cold February, and his Father is present at birth. His parents got separated; they have only been married for about a year. The little boy lives with his mother.

A Mother, that has been wounded from her childhood. A spiritual infection that cannot make cured. Injuries can become infected; bitterness is contagious, and many can be infected by it. Wounds from a childhood. In a world full of impressions. From the outside, a boy like all other boys, from the inside a wound open to infection. An injury inside, and for pain, as he learned to hide. Who is open to whom? Who's to blame, for his situation? Who is to blame when the upbringing is to blame? Or is it the devil; Satan, the prosecutor, the splitter, and the evil speaker?

An obsession takes the form of showing the world the finger.

All sins begins in the small. A little hole in a wall eventually tears the whole wall down open to everything and everyone. He shut himself up, encapsulated. Psychoanalysis will fall short, or the study of what's going on inside the head. Where do the thoughts come from it? Can you discern what you can see?

Then comes the teens, darkness is soaked in, because he has decided. He has made up his mind. Deciding on a given direction is his choice without apology. A life without meaning begins to take shape, a choice, and it is no longer meaningless to him. He did not receive the light because the darkness in him did not comprehend it. Obsession is now complete. Possessed from obsession is to give, "Love a bad name."

Love will grow cold in most people, assuming they have had the love.

A man on the verge of madness, and multiplied is pretty many. Like a man, Jesus Christ met: "He was possessed of the devil and became healed." What a human can do if it is receptive of good and evil,

this man who put everything in order. In an obsession of being possessed.

Possessed; Greek Word; Daemon; a supernatural spirit; Be vexed with it; Be possessed with it.

To be possessed is to be controlled with something or someone.

Only daring to write about obsession can be on the verge of madness.

In modern times everything has to be explained. Call it darkness, the dark side of a human being. Philosophy does the same. But set aside the philosophy. Occupation of being possessed, then it is a word that comes to mind, and it is; control of mind. Where do the thoughts come from it?

The man is now entering into adulthood. Empowered enough to be responsible for everything he intends to do. He made a choice, and with his occupation, he is implementing the fatal from a child to a terrorist. He was possessed by thought, from hatred to action.

July 22, 2011, the Norwegian terrorist unleashed an approximately 1,000-kilogram bomb. In the government quarter and conducting a massacre against a political youth camp on an island in one of Norway's largest lakes, many people killed.

After the trial, the sentence becomes 21 years in custody. After the verdict comes the big question. No remorse found, no repentance.

Had it been an obsession, he would have repented, and regret after one foot out and the other after it.

But instead, he chooses to stand firm on what he has done and openly proclaims that he wants to study Political Science in prison and he will sit there for a long time. From obsession to being possessed. With no remorse.

Everything is very well until that day; the grandiose mirror image is made blurred. That is to say, everything in your atmosphere is shaking. Don't blame everyone it's you to blame. Evil is still evil, and a shovel is still a shovel because you are receptive. At the root of the word narcissism, everything is corrupt. With self-righteousness and pride. Narcissism in a closet you have to get out of.

The story of a little boy in a well:
Several years earlier, after accepting Jesus Christ as my Lord and Savior. I was asked to join a Cafe in the church

I attended, a Cafe with a large kitchen. A Cafe open to people of all kinds. A Cafe open to people who do not usually attend the church service. Where people could get dinner without paying, eventually, it became a meeting point for people. Where they could feel at home, here came all kinds of people. From people with poor economics. Substance abusers, people with mental problems, unstable, wholly obsessed people, a Cafe with a variety of people, like Jesus Christ walked within his days. In the church of God, it is open to all but to repentance.

Then one day, a young boy came in. He was in his twenties, and enter the door with a low threshold for all kinds of people he sat down first and foremost, with a quiet but observant look.

When I sit down with him for a pleasant visit, he manifests himself. Eventually, he becomes a regular guest. Every time we are open, he comes by. We leave him until he starts to be naughty and nasty to some of our female employees—partly scary behavior—obsessed scares, especially when someone is possessed.

A male employee takes the young boy aside, and correct him. There is a disgusting presence present.

In light of the truth, a young man shows up just to create disorder, a dominant personality that is divisive.

After being rebuked and explained to him, we close the Cafe for the evening, and take for granted that he has taken the warning seriously. Hopefully he will behave better the next time we open the Cafe.

A beautiful spring day a week later after the incident. I am going in the morning to prepare the Cafe for an opening—cooking, etc. Then I see this young man standing outside the front door. He smiles obsessively, saying only a few words. His whole being makes me think he has something in store. Like he's trying to put me out of the games—a dominant nature. I'm taking a step forward smiles, look at him and ask: "What's your name, actually?». A person with a split personality smiles smartly and says briefly: "Daemon."

Then I look deep into his eyes with peace. Suddenly, his dark brown eyes open to a deep funnel. In the end, I see a little boy frightened, stretching his arms up towards me. Like someone has fallen into a well and not able to get up from there with a desperate look, and a desire to be saved. When I saw this vision in this young man I will never forget.

Later, this man was taken care of by psychiatry in the closed ward—a potential threat to society and lobotomized with powerful drugs, controlled with medical treatment, in an institution with science that falls short. The only thing I saw was a desperate boy with a desire to be saved. Deep down in a well with no ability to get up.

A story of Mary Magdalene:

Who was Mary Magdalene?

What does the Bible say about Mary Magdalene?

Other than that, Jesus Christ set her free from seven demons; Daemon. She was the first to meet Jesus Christ after His resurrection at the grave.

One day Jesus was invited by Simon a Pharisee to his home, and Jesus came and behold, a woman in the city who was a sinner, and a culprit. (Sin; One who missed the mark, and so does not share in the prize). She entered the Pharisee's house when she knew Jesus was there, boldly.

«She brought an alabaster box of ointment, and stood at His feet behind Him weeping, and began to wash His feet with tears, and wiped them with the hairs of her head, and kissed His fed, and anointed them with the ointment."

The Pharisees called her a sinner and could not understand why Jesus let her touch him. A woman probably a prostitute or at least frivolous lives a life outside the framework of the Pharisees, and outside the Law of Moses. An outdated law decayed in the dark outside the light God Almighty had set. No joy. Just a law.

The story doesn't use her name to be any woman, any culprit, or another similar story where Mary, with the same first name, did the same. Mary, sister of Lazarus who Jesus raised from the dead. She also anointed the feet of Jesus Christ with ointment. Very costly. In eternal gratitude for what Jesus had done for her brother. Which was also present, vibrant.

Mary Magdalene, with the same eternal gratitude for being set free from seven demons. From possessed and under control to freedom. She owed everything to Jesus Christ. She was weeping with joy at what Jesus Christ had done.

«And a certain woman who has been healed of evil spirits and infirmities, Mary Magdalene, out of whom went seven devils…»

She was with him now and ministered to him of her substance. So grateful. In gratitude for being lifted by the well, she made trapped in it. Desperate arms lifted, and Jesus Christ, with power over demons, set her free from her captivity. This story of a woman anointed His feet with her hair. An act of love and humility that only lies in pure love. A story from Simons's house. The Pharisee made shown a real person with a sincere heart. The name Mary Magdalene is not mentioned, but her attitude towards Jesus Christ makes it clear that she must have known Him before, and for that reason she followed Jesus Christ throughout every city and village, as He preached the joyful message. The glad tidings. The Gospel of the Kingdom of God.

In my revelation, none other than Mary Magdalene was in Simon's house.

«Verily I say unto you, Wheresoever this gospel shall be preached in the whole world shall also this, that this woman hath done, be told for a memorial of her.»
 It is a reminder for us to see clearly what Jesus Christ can do.

We must get out of our own opinion: Jesus Christ is the way, the truth, and the life. These three words are interconnected and can't live apart. They are one.
The Way; Mary Magdalene followed Jesus Christ wherever He went.
Truth; set her free from seven demons, and a sinful life.
Life; it was the one she chose after meeting Jesus Christ. She lived out her faith as a testimony to the whole world. Over faithfulness to conviction, one who was much forgiven and loved a lot. Love has no place on a weighted balanced bowl, because it loves, despite everything.

I see the freedom of the word hardship. Tribulation, because it's something you have to go through. Not the freedom of the expression tribulation itself, but freedom behind it.
Jesus Christ was alone during the entire crucifixion. Right until the resurrection.
But there is a resistance, and it can make found in the splitter to divide and separate something from each other. But in the aftermath of what Jesus Christ had to go through. After meeting the disciples He shows them the

freedom of being in Jesus Christ, and the freedom there is to sit at the Father's Right hand.

If you know the freedom and believe in it, the privilege will be present even in tribulation.

In Acts, Apostle Peter and other Apostles are both beaten and imprisoned. They praised the Lord Almighty. Freedom and joy that does despite pain and fear. Since there is no fear in love, «but perfect love casteth out fear: because of fear hath torment. He that feareth is not made perfect in love».

Do we know the word of God, we recognize what we read, from revelation.

Love is no longer «Despite everything» but only love based on what we recognize in it. Seeing the world from our point of view is a dangerous starting point. There love, will grow cold, unless you have much forgiven and been able to love a lot.

Freedom under obedience.

«For the weapons of our warfare are not carnal, but mighty through God to the pulling down of strongholds; Casting down imaginations, and every high thing that exalteth itself against the knowledge of God, and bringing into captivity every thought to the obedience of Christ;…»

«Where do the thoughts come from?» It made it put into a philosophical question mark: Even the question itself captures the captivity.

I've seen people trapped by their work, and all their energy, and mindset bound into it, they made a choice.

«… and bringing into captivity every thought to the obedience …».

Philosophy means; love of knowledge. They submit to the thoughts: And not under obedience to Jesus Christ. Obedience is a revolutionary word of freedom. «For the weapons of our warfare are not carnal, but mighty through God to the pull-down of strongholds; …». In the freedom front, you stand on the barricades, «Casting down imaginations, and every high thing that exalteth itself against the knowledge of God, …».

It is not the «French Revolution» or«The Black Fight for Freedom in the United States» or «Woman's Liberation» for that matter.

All of this is rooted in a desire to claim what others have. «Fight for your right …». Humanism; Human welfare. Freedom; Mary Magdalene followed Jesus wherever He went because she was free. Under obedience to Jesus Christ. She made given the ability to think for herself. After being freed from «Seven Devils.»

Freedom is not necessarily peace but a sword. Sword; a synonymous word for battle. Obedience is a weapon, and we are bringing into captivity every thought under obedience to Christ. We are not free; Indeed, before any thought made captured; In Christ.

Jeremiah, one Prophet once said to the Israelites people: «For I know the thoughts that I think toward you, saith the Lord, thoughts of peace, and not of evil, to give you an expected end.»
Thoughts of Peace; from Hebrew, shalom; a primitive root; to be safe (in mind, body or estate).

Jeremiah told a disobedient people; they were taken captive by the enemy, and it lasted for 70 years.
Peace thoughts can make found at the Humanist. In the congregation, and there they sit well. Peace thoughts are capturing thoughts under obedience to Jesus Christ. Get up and out, on the barricades to break down the fortifications. Strive to enter the narrow gate. That is freedom and peace with God Almighty.

Religions are captivity, and they don't capture thoughts of the mind.

Karl Marx, the revolutionary forerunner of communism, once said: «It is not the religions that have created the people. But the human who has created the religions».
Karl Marx made the fatal mistake; he captured his mind, "bringing into captivity every thought,"; that under the

circumstances, there is no Almighty God and Creator.
Beyond everything.
In other words, his fortifications made him strong. His
fortifications were carnal. A revolutionary rooted in
philosophical thought, when freedom is not present, simply rooted in its conception.

Then we are back where we started, "The Fall of Man",
it persecutes us. Right to the end. Without «capturing any
thought under obedience to Christ», God does not favor
disobedience.
Even if the thought seems like good—thoughts of peace.

The word obedience is not captivity, on the contrary.
Put our eyes in the light. What do we see? Grand
Canyon? Or a polluted metropolis?
The word obedience; under obedience to Jesus Christ,
we are made from Potter's hand. Never forget it. In His
Image. Not an evolutionary Big Bang Theory. That de-
velops us to become independent individuals—an evolution of independence.
Obedience; to hear under (as a subordinate); to listen at-
tentively; by implication, to heed or conform to a command or authority;-hearken, be obedient to, obey.
Or say it simple; Hearken; hear, and listen on whichever
level we are able.
The only evolution I'm sticking to is: Developing an
ability to listen more. «Under obedience to Jesus Christ.»

Thoughts of peace, and not evil, give you an expected end, says the Lord. «Then shall ye call upon me, and ye shall go and pray unto me, and I will hearken unto you.».
Hearken Hebrew; Shama; to hear intelligently. There is a freedom to listen intelligently.
Have you ever been in the wilderness? In a forest? In pristine nature. Have you been surrounded by your thoughts? Well, I have.
Then you stop and push your mind away, and start to hear. The foliage hisses in the wind. The birds are tweeting. The brook chimes quietly. The more you listen, the more sounds you hear. You are online, connected.
Here comes freedom, intelligently. God answers you. You just have to listen. Have Faith, trust fully.
I have never experienced more freedom than when God Almighty hears me.
Strive to enter the narrow gate, and you will. Be hearken, intelligently.
It is no more liberating than hearing to "hearken."

Animal Farm by George Orwell.
Animal Farm is an allegorical novella published in England on August 17, 1945.
The book tells the story of a group of farm animals who rebels against their human farmer (call it Capitalism). They were hoping to create a society where animals can be equal, free, and happy. Ultimately, however, the rebellion is betrayed. The farm ends up in a state as bad as it

was before, under the dictatorship of a pig named
Napoleon (call the pig Communism).
It is a political satire. Based on reality. Humans being a
fight for their rights, and become animals.

They have arguments for everything, and not interested
in submitting to an Almighty God. What so ever; To
submit is free will to obedience.

Oppression to Submit. We become rebellious against rebelliousness; We fight for our rights.
There are no Isms with total freedom.
 -Ism is a suffix in many English words. It means «taking
side with» or «imitation of,» and is often used to describe philosophies, theories, religions, social movements, artistic meanings, and behaviors.
Then freedom under obedience to Christ came to a brief.
We don't know always what we're doing, or say. We do
what is right, assuming it suits us.
Looking for the truth can be the needle in the high
stakes. So what do we do? Repentance, change direction.
Take any thoughts in captivity.
«Casting down imaginations, and every high thing that
exalteth itself against the knowledge of God, and bringing into captivity every thought to the obedience of
Christ;…»

Devil; The Invisible man.

The one who destroys and kills

«The thief cometh not, but for to steal, kill, and destroy:…»

And you can't see it.

Almost every unbeliever I meet, end up in an argument that; if God exists, why does He accept all the evil in this world?

This thought has to come from the same source, and not an individual opinion on behalf of some circumstances. Try to find the source beyond everything, and you will discover hardware behind it. A person, with no limit. To destroy means; to totally ruin; to destroy fully, and it starts with a thought.

Satan, which is the father of all lies is obsessed to destroy, kill, create divisions and accusation. Satan will create havoc wherever he gains access. The one who split, accuse, and the father of all lies.

He is not free; he pretends to be.

Jesus Christ is Freedom, in all its simplicity.

Christ took all our sins, on the cross. By His Father in Heaven, rises again on the third day, defeated death and Satan. Proclaim to have the key to the kingdom of death, and eternal life for those who trustfully have faith, with faithfulness.

To repent is to change direction from our past. To Jesus Christ, because we chose to walk wrong way He had to die on the cross, crucified, and be able to release us from the world snares. This is Almighty God recovery for the man created in His image.

In His rest.

"In His Rest"
What does rest mean? The body's rest? (Is it a preconception in the word rest? Or prejudice?).
«Come unto me, all you that labor …». Labor; is to feel fatigued and to work hard in a wearied way.
«…, and are heavy laden, …». When you are loaded up with heavy laden. In His rest means to come to an end. Do not make it more difficult than it is.
It is to pick words and phrases apart, and put them back together. Primary words can often be lost, also revelations, and it never stops.

I was at a Christian gathering once. They took some bricks on a foundation wall, and then ripped off parts of it again. The picture I saw, was a useless foundation wall where it was not possible to build a house. A house without the opportunity to rest on a foundation wall; therefore, the old foundation wall must be gone, to make a new one. The Bible uses pictures of us as a Holy Temple. So a building. A temple must make built on a foundation wall. Holy meant when the Almighty God is the foundation wall. Established, through Jesus Christ.

«Come unto me, all ye that labor and are heavily laden, and I will give you rest. Take my yoke upon you, and learn of me; for I am meek and lowly in heart: and ye shall find rest unto your souls, for my yoke is easy, and my burden is light».

Lowly; of uncertain derivation; depressed, Jesus Christ takes your depression. He put Himself in your position. Because He says: «Lean on Me.» Because He is, meek and lowly in heart, and you will find rest unto your heart/soul: Spirit; heart.

A foundation wall is not a facade, but a facade who can rest on it so that it can remain standing. Standing means you are capable of walking.

«For we are His workmanship, created in Christ Jesus unto good works, which God hath before ordained that we should walk in them.»

Ordained; to fit up in advance, ordain before, prepare afore. Make ready.

«…we should walk»; walk at large. Be occupied with; tread (down) underfoot, which means a path.

Ready-made, deeds; is not a qualified understanding: It can end up in; do not do because it is ready. To build a road is not for «ready.» But for walking.

Structural engineers say: «The most complicated thing you can build is a road.» Jesus says: «I am the way, the

truth, and the life …». Way; road; path. It was ordained for you to walk on it. To be used.
Whether we are in the world's hammock or strive for your gain, here we do not find "In His Rest."
Everyone has a language; language comes naturally; we rest; while we talk. The Bible warns us not to be left behind. From His Rest. We are no longer in the old covenant, under the Law of Moses, but under the new covenant in Jesus Christ. With a law written in our hearts, what I did before I could no longer do. My sin searched—my conscience.

We can see many Christians living a life more as like the world, than to disciple, like Jesus Christ.
What the world offers they have taken. They have made flesh weak, in their defense. But they do not have the Freedom to be set free. They cultivate their weaknesses. They defend themselves, and what they see is a religious figure they call Jesus Christ. Welcome to the world's Roller coaster, not to rest in God's Almighty peace. Just a peace built on emotional life. Like the world.

Bible says: «Therefore, since a promise remains of entering His rest, let us fear lest any of you should seem to have come short of it.»
Come short of it; meaning, to fall short, fail, or left behind.
Is there Freedom in being talked to it?

123

From Potter's hand, we are His vessels He rules, and judge righteously. In the freedom of Christ we can rest in Him.

«Submit yourselves therefore to God. Resist the devil, and he will flee from you».
Flee; to run away, to shun; by analogy, to vanish:-escape. Devil will run, not walk. Flee; escape. This word also means the word fear. Flee and fear. They live together like a defenseless wild animal. In other words, he is no longer Predator, you are. You are now at the top of the ranking ladder, a role change. That's why you resist him, and submit yourselves to God.
Synonyms: Escape—Runaway from a place or situation of danger.
The synonyms for; to flee; run for it, and to take to one's heals, make retreat.

In Asia somewhere, I almost stepped on a cobra snake. To scare it away, I trampled into the ground, loud and clear. Then it took to one's heel and disappeared. The devil does not necessarily give up. He only finds someone else who can't resist him, and who don't submit themselves to God Almighty, and Jesus Christ.
Put it in order: You have to draw near to Him first. Jesus Christ will draws near to you, because you have submitted to Him first.
Don't underestimate the devil, but resist him.

The word «flee from you» is more powerful than you can imagine when Jesus Christ is near you.

«Let not your heart be troubled: ye believe in God, also believe in Me.» Jesus Christ includes Himself.

Jesus Christ is «the way, the truth, and the life: no man cometh unto the Father, but by Me.» He closes up any other options, and with His Peace, we may be in His Rest. The Peace God gives a promise to rest in Him. New foundation wall for a Holy Temple. Lean on Him and devil will flee; run away from you, in a hurry. Trust in God and trust in Me has the keyword for the devil to escape from us. But be aware he can always "Return to sender" and, to resist is to stand against.

When Mary Magdalene was set free, she followed Jesus Christ wherever He went. She was free to go, independent of this world.

Today I see women have been to Calvary, accept Jesus as Lord and Savior, and end up in a church where they get their permanent place. Mary Magdalene's heart stagnates into something they "think" they made called to. Or husbands make them busy with household chores, and the burning desire to follow Jesus Christ end up in a religiosity without the Freedom to follow Him. Do not become a woman of the world liberates, but free to follow one with Freedom's promise Freedom.

Do you know that Jesus Christ is the first woman liberator in the world? Many women followed Him-all the way to the grave, and were the first to see Jesus' resurrection. Do not underestimate yourself, just because you are a woman. Christ did not give them rights, but through his actions made them humble enough to follow Him. Just as we will resist the devil, so God Almighty stands against the proud today. As many proud women liberators today are; To women who have chosen to follow Jesus Christ. Do not continue to be an infant, but independent from worlds opinion, stand up—walk-in His ready-made deeds.

Leaders in the churches call themselves shepherds, well, Jesus washed the disciples' feet. He taught the disciples equality. The woman in Paradise was created as a helper comparable of man. Before the man became "the woman's head." Jesus restores Paradise before the "Fall of Man." Let the Pastors get down from the pulpit, and let them be the shepherd they proclaim to be. It is not rebellion, but the way the church should be.

When lies told many times close to the truth, we choose to believe it. Get yourself (Women) up and out to what you are passionate about for Christ in Freedom, having been to Calvary after being Born Again.
Calvary; if we have not personally experienced in our hearts the place where Jesus Christ crucified for our

wounds, what He did for us on the cross, indeed. Are we also not able to experience the Freedom of Jesus Christ? Freedom when Jesus gave his life on a cross. To win back a lost world. Calvary is the meeting place where you meet Jesus Christ. Without Calvary, you cannot know Jesus, neither acknowledges and confesses.

If you want to have a right relationship with Christ, you must admit - to Jesus Christ, personally.

Strive to enter the narrow strait gate involving Calvary. Calvary, where Jesus Christ crucified.

Calvary; a skull (cranium). A place "where they crucified Him, and the malefactors, one on the right hand, and the others on the left." Malefactors mean wrongdoing, criminal: - evildoer. Apparently a primary word; worthlessness.

Calvary means suffering Jesus Christ made wounded for our sins. All whom I had met those who were "Born Again" in Water and Spirit, they have been on the path of suffering, imprisioned in Fowler's Net, a painful experience.

A man came to Jesus Christ, at night. He was not free enough to go during the day; Jesus let him in. His name was Nicodemus. A scholar, one with knowledge. However, not with insight, since he did not understand when Jesus Christ said, that he must be "Born Again." One who could not know that the law must be written in his heart, soul, and not into his head, in intellectual captivity.

"Jesus answered, Verily, verily, I say unto thee, Except a man be born of water and the Spirit, he cannot enter into the kingdom of God."

He was getting into Mom's life once again, a physical understanding from Nicodemus. Jesus Christ said: We are to understand everything in "Spirit and Truth." In Revelation. Nicodemus was not there yet. Only because he was not "Born Again." Dare to believe was something new for him, a religious Pharisee, one that came at night. Because he was not "Born Again," and not yet feared for nothing, and however had no revelations about God's Almighty Word. He did not yet have the primary deeper meaning of The Word of God. As Jesus Christ said to him (Nicodemus): "Are you the teacher of Israel, and do not know these things? ".

Nicodemus was not aware of, not perceived, or resolved it into an understanding of knowledge of God Almighty. Only an intellectual understanding was told by others and into his "Time of Age." Frequently the word "Born Again" was far away from his knowledge, and yet not revealed.

Not like the prophets in the Old Testament. Listen to what the Prophet says and hearken it:

"And I will give them one heart, and put a new spirit within you; and I will take the stony heart out of their flesh, and will give them a heart of flesh: That they walk in My statutes, and keep My ordinances, and do them: and they shall be My people, and I will be their God. "

A Prophet which has The Spirit from God; a foretells an inspired speaker; a Poet.

Did you know that Father Almighty God also is Father of Poem?

Imagine someone is trapped in: Into religions, religiosity, doctrines, some Ism. They lost their opportunity to have an open mind. God Almighty said: "Let there be light, and there was light. " It can't be more Poem than that-Freedom to see.

"Let there be light... ".

Nicodemus overthought, so he sought Jesus, at night. Heresy is not necessarily what is said, but also what one omits to mention—false prophet, religious impostor, who generates to toast on a wrong basis. Our perceptions take up a lot of space, it occupies, you have to clean away, to make room for something new. Bury the old, upright with something new. Nicodemus experienced it. Since he was embalming Jesus Christ after Jesus crucified, he became a man of God Almighty, and no longer in a religion. To make a heart of flesh, pray in Spirit and truth. A promise from Jesus Christ before He left the Earth.

"But the hour cometh, and now is, when the true worshippers shall worship the Father in Spirit and truth: for the Father seeketh such to worship him.

God is a Spirit: and they that worship him must worship him in Spirit and truth ".

129

In Greek philosophy, they say that your truth is not necessarily my truth. The fact can be taken apart by saying, "What is truth?" Asking a question is synonymous with doubt, and do not believe.

The truth today is often misunderstood as to what is right. The truth alone can be convincing, or put everything in doubt by saying, "What is truth?". A question can make a distinction between perceptions, dissension. Or put the person in doubt with a question?

A truth cannot live alone without Spirit. The Holy Spirit, the one who guides leads us to the fact. Therefore, we must be born again. Accordingly, Nicodemus questioned the truth. By asking Jesus how he could return to Mother's womb when Jesus Christ said he had to be "born again." In Water and Spirit, without the Holy Spirit, no truth.

When Jesus answer anyone who ask question about the truth: "For this cause I was born, and for this cause I have come into the world, that I should bear witness to the truth. Everyone who is of the truth hears My voice." Being of the Holy Spirit is truth. A promise made; to get a New Heart, and a New Spirit instead of a stony heart. He will be our God; They walk in My Statues, and keep My ordinances, and do them.

Only a heart of flesh, New Heart, can love our enemy— the word enemy; to hate. So if you have an enemy, you hate them. Or if you hate someone, you have an enemy. Bible says, if you hate a "brother", you are a murderer.

In Beatitudes, Jesus Christ teaches us to love everyone. To do this, you must have a Heart of Flesh and not a stony heart. Be born again. Nicodemus came at night, to hear Jesus Christ say, "For this is the condemnation, that light has come into the world, and men loved darkness rather than light because their deeds were evil. Because he that doeth truth come to light, that his deeds may manifest, that they wrought revealed, in God ". Unbelief is the same as disobedience. Nicodemus chose to come to Jesus, but at night. Once and for all because he was not "In His Rest," yet. That night Nicodemus learned more than the rest of his life. He listened intelligently and did not take Jesus Christ for granted, obviously.

Being born again includes the Holy Spirit. It is of God and cannot sin. Neither goes into the yoke with sin. "Blessed are the pure in heart: for they shall see God. " Therefore, God could no longer walk with Adam and his like, Eve. They were no longer pure in heart, to eat the fruit from the Tree of Knowledge, good and evil, a disobedient act, to sin. Being "born again" does not prevent us from falling into sin. "And grieve not the Holy Spirit of God, ...". Means: We hinder the work of God, takes sin lightly. No revelations, and gives the devil room so that we separated from the Freedom we could have been in it—the Freedom to be in the service of an Almighty

God. To walk in the yoke is religious. Almighty God cannot go into the yoke with something unclean. Repentance is all needed since the law made written in our hearts.

Do not be discouraged. But believe in the promises Jesus Christ has promised us. Spirit of fear makes you depressed. In His Rest, you find Peace. In God's Peace, you will find Freedom. "Peace I leave with you, My Peace I give unto you: not as the world giveth, give I unto you. Let not your heart be troubled, neither let it be afraid," says Jesus Christ. The word Troubled also means; revolt. Put in a revolt.

Jesus' blood is the basis for the new purity as it removes the guilt of sin and creates a unique inner purity. Blessed are the pure in heart: for they shall see God. Seeing God Almighty is Freedom. Pure at heart, to walk with Him. In all things. Being "born again" enables you to walk in spiritual matters. Seeing God Almighty, you will die. Physically, no one can enter into God. Nor in impurity, to be complete with Him. In the form of Jesus Christ, been to Calvary. On the path of suffering in humility and sorrow, over the sin of this world. To be embraced in God's Almighty divine atmosphere. In His Rest, to walk entirely with Him. With knowledge, we fall short. Only with the revelations of wisdom. Can you walk into this? Jesus Christ is present. By grace alone, I was allowed to enter, and God Almighty shines on that which is pure.

The old in me must die. Upright with something new. Be born again.

Justice, judgment, and equity:
Righteous, originally means "to be pure" and has a legal meaning: "to be acquitted, innocent." What more could Freedom want? The right is strait (ness). Righteous, and not unstable in all his ways, do not doubt.
"Blessed are they which are persecuted for righteousness' sake: for theirs is the kingdom of heaven, "for righteousness sake. With Jesus Christ, we must declare ourselves guilty. To be recognized as innocent, and get clean.
"Many shall be purified and made white and tried, but the wicked shall do wickedly, and none of the wicked shall understand, but the wise shall understand. "
Purified is to clarify cleanse and polished. Be pure.

Righteousness; there are no cowards or a timid in Father Almighty's Heaven. Timid; showing a lack of courage or confidence; easily frightened. Faithless: - fearful.
"And there shall be no wise enter into it anything that defileth, neither whatsoever worked abomination, or maketh a lie, but they which are written in the Lambs book of life. "
Defiled; is unclean, unholy, and it will be common, because a little leaven leavens the hole lump.

The unclean will ferment the New earth and New heaven, which promised. Like first Adam under this earth, with disobedient and sin, eat from the Tree of Knowledge. Righteousness is the keyword to fit into the Lamb's book of life, which is Jesus Christ. No one comes to the Father except true Him. Jesus says: "Be perfect as the Father in Heaven is perfect." For us, this is a daily working process. Not a promise. Perfect; a complete man or woman with the mental and moral character of full age. With labor and growth, all this can be done in His Rest. Rest while walking in peace, with God Almighty.

"At this time, Jesus answered and said, I thank thee, O Father, Lord of Heaven and earth, because thou hast hid these things from the wise and prudent, and hast revealed them unto babes. "

Babes not speaking, a simple-minded infant person. An immature Christian, a child.

A child is one who is ready to grow up. Father in heaven can't use those who are already grown up's. Simply because they fully booked in their mind, useless; Worthless. A humble-minded child is what God Almighty needs. Trustfully without any question. Ready to follow Almighty Father. In Jesus Christ's name. Jesus showed his disciples what was possible. He showed faith in works, in His Rest, anything we can do, to do. Not a hearer only but a doer. A doer is a performer; Poet. Speak is to Do.

One day, Fowler's net is your testimony. Your Freedom can make proclaimed to others, with Jesus Christ through you. You can redeem others out of their snares. You have become a child who is allowed to grow, and In His Rest. When "Our soul escaped as a bird out of the snare of the fowlers: the snare is broken, and we are escaped"; is my soul spiritually since the primitive root of the soul; to breathe passively, to make breathed upon it. We were refreshed as if by a current of air. To be restored from your labor and heavy burden. As Jesus Christ's yoke is easy, and His burden is light.

Some say that God's ministry is hard work, but without; In His Rest, it will be in your command. Jesus Christ knew His labor. So let us follow Him and not ourselves into another Fowler's net. Again.
Some say; it's all by grace, through Jesus Christ. But without the law written in your Heart and soul, your grace is in vain, and you can not rest without it. The law is only there and able to distinguish between right and wrong, injustice, and justice. Justice causes judgment and equity. Without being "Born Again," you will get nowhere. "In your place of standing" to put it that way. The apostle Paul puts it this way: "And this I pray, that your love may abound more and more in knowledge and all judgment; That ye may approve things that are excellent; that ye may be sincere and without offense till the day of Christ; ... "

135

Knowledge means; full discernment. For yourself and to others, discernment a tool from God Almighty to make released. Like it was in The Beginning when God Almighty created us "..., and He saw it was good". Paul also continues, "...; Being filled with the fruits of right-eousness, which are by Jesus Christ, unto the glory and praise of God". An innocent, clean, and holy person.

I have had faith; I have had unbelief or lack of faith. What do I choose? Where does the road go next? I have learned one thing; the biggest obstacle in my life has been myself. I did what I was not supposed to do, and what I was going to do, I did not do. Remember one thing: For some, you never do enough. For others, you do not need to do anything. What Jesus Christ wants is that you walk with Him. Like Mary Magdalene; wherev-er Christ goes. Get to know Him so that you do not fall into your traps or snare.
Jesus Christ said: "And then I will profess unto them; I never knew you: depart from me, ye that work iniquity." Walk with Jesus Christ. How Adam and Eve walked with God Almighty before The Fall of Man. To know some-one, you have to walk with them, present. I write to my-self and others, because I have something to say, loud and clear. So do you. To do is to Speak. To others. But then you have to go out to others. Paradise's test of obe-dience was not to eat of the Tree of knowledge of good and evil. To obey Jesus Christ, is to love God Almighty

with all your heart, and your neighbor as yourselves, in this laying the Great Commandment: "Go out to all nations" because we made unto good works. By grace, through Faith. Be released into Freedom, and you will see The Light, which is Jesus Christ-divided from the dark side, of the moon. Our Universe is mostly dark without the light.

I will shine upon you, Jesus Christ says, and give you rest. But before you go out somewhere, you have to go into something first. Go into your inner room, shut the door, shut your mind from all disturbances seek Him in secret, and the Father in Heaven who sees you in secret shall reward you openly.

"Stand therefore in the liberty wherewith Christ hath made us free, and be not entangled again with a yoke of bondage."

In liberty, we have Freedom wherewith Christ has made us free, and not entangled in an ensnare again. We made yoked in Fowler's net of bondage. Father in heaven will reward you openly. Stand, therefore, solid.

Jesus said unto self-righteous religious Pharisee; "They that are whole have no need of a physician but they that are sick: I came not to call the righteous, but sinners to repentance." The primary word of sick is worthless; a sinner who missed the mark. It is us in all humbleness. Jesus Christ is my Lord and Savior. He cannot fail; we can. Freedom is not independent, but to rely on Him. Those who have been near Jesus Christ knows.

Do you feel the emptiness? In vain, then you are not in Freedom. In the future, one can probably download the Freedom in a robot, and it will act like it is free, but is not to dream of escape from something.

It's an adventure to find true Freedom; It's not an Idol. It's not a fairy tale. It's real. It's Jesus Christ. A fortune. A great Commandment, "Go ye out to all the world, ...", can't be more Freedom than that, and surely, Christ will set you free.

Fear is not Freedom. Not in a yoke with thoughts either. Freedom believes in All things. Based on the Truth, and what Jesus Christ says:

"If the Son, therefore, shall make you free, ye shall be free indeed."

Receive Jesus Christ as you should, one foot out and the other after, you will not regret it. "Strive to enter the narrow strait gate." He will release you from the snare His yoke and burden are light. One day you will discover that Fowler's net was only part of the chapter of your life. Remember you will receive revelation about the entire content of the Bible which means; Books: "Be in me, and I will Be in you," Quote Jesus Christ.

Epilogue

A midwife does not give birth. She's just helping to release the baby, from Mother. She arranges everything for the delivery without complications. When the water goes, the child is on his way, out. Biblical redemption is the revelation of God's Word, nothing else. Explaining God's Almighty Word is one thing. Redeeming the Word of God Almighty is a revelation. Jesus' parables made given to the disciples, to listen to understand, with heart. That which comes out of itself. When the water goes. Revelation.

There was no pastor or any Christian to my redemption. It was a longing to know Him, and He did not come. Only after "Strive to enter the strait gate" Jesus Christ did. No one told me what to do. It is only the midwife in the Spirit of God for guidance, and revelation. When the baby is delivered, it can take place in the Mother's arms to become bosom. Jesus compares the Kingdom of God to a hen gathering her chickens under her wings. For protection and training, for guidance. It is us in Christ, and Christ in us. "Behold, I stand at the door, and knock: if any man hears my voice and opens the door, I will come into him and will sup with him, and he with me."

The Bible says: "For my thoughts are not your thoughts, neither are your ways my ways, saith the Lord, for as the heavens are higher than the earth, so are my ways higher than your ways, and my thoughts than your thoughts."
We must do what Mary Magdalene did. She followed Him wherever He went, also spiritually. In gratitude for being released, the snare.
"Our soul is escaped as a bird out of the snare of the fowlers: the snare is broken, and we are escaped. Our help is in the name of the Lord, who made heaven and earth."
Follow Him, and no one else. Except for those who followed Jesus Christ. They followed Him together, with the same mind, with equal redemption.
No one should make Jesus Christ a philosopher. He is the only begotten Son of God. For redemption.
A birth to strive, to enter the narrow gate, and He redeem us from Fowler's net.

PS:
Please do not made my
testimony and revelation which is given,
to an doctrine.
But given for release.
Because a doctrine is a snare.

Christ - Your Healer

On a tree, He hung
On a tree, it happened
the manipulators thought
it was the centuries
biggest bang

Christ arose
the beautiful third day
cause death could not
tear Him apart

Christ is the love Himself
reach out for it now
and be brought
out of the manipulator's shelf

Believe in His work
believe in His love

cause the calvary shows
the truth beyond doubt

What need's to be done
is to repent to Christ
the only giver of
freedom and life

From that day on
once again you will be born
this is called spiritual reborn
but now in Christ
not after Satan's heist

Jesus Christ
loves you so much
that's what it's all about

God bless you so much!